Sea Kayaking Canada's West Coast

John Ince & Hedi Köttner

THE MOUNTAINEERS
Seattle

THE MOUNTAINEERS: Organized in 1906 ". . . to explore, study, preserve and enjoy the natural beauty of the Northwest."

Published in the United States by The Mountaineers
1011 SW Klickitat Way, Seattle, Washington 98134

Published simultaneously in Canada by Raxas Books, Inc.,
1103-207 W. Hastings St., Vancouver, B.C. V6B 1H7

Manufactured in Canada

All photographs taken by the authors unless otherwise credited.
Editing by Galiano Wordcraft, Galiano Island, B.C.
Cartography by Phil Magnall, Richmond, B.C.
Layout by Orca Sound Design, Vancouver, B.C.
Design by Ince/Kottner Consultants, Inc., Vancouver, B.C.

Front cover: Bella Bella area
Title spread: Knight Inlet
Back cover: Brooks Peninsula, west coast of Vancouver Island

ISBN 0-89886-342-2 (US)

Dedication

to Shirley and Geoff Ince
to Maria and Gerlinde Kottner

Table of Contents

Acknowledgements

Many thanks to the scores of kayakers, fishermen, pleasure boaters, native people, float plane pilots, loggers, wilderness outfitters (notably Ecosummer Expeditions, Kanawa Expeditions and the Strathcona Park Lodge), conservation groups and others who have so generously shared with us their knowledge of the coast.

Special thanks to Mark Peckham who accompanied us on many of our paddling ventures and to all of the other paddlers who made our trips so much fun.

We are deeply indebted to the following people who read the manuscript or portions of it and offered valuable advice and suggestions: Jim Allan, Herb Davies, John Dowd, Heather Harbord, Mary Morris, Leroy Nordby, Nick Rebalski, David Smith, Bob Sutherland and Marilyn Winterbottom. Special thanks to Leroy Nordby for his comments about kayak kiting, contained in Appendix A.

Finally, we are grateful to all the people who worked on the production of the book, and to Gordon Soules for his guidance and enthusiasm.

How to Use This Book

This book is divided into two parts. Part I outlines the west coast paddling environment: the weather, the sea, the flora and fauna, and the cultural setting of the coast. Part I also describes the equipment you will need to outfit a paddling cruise.

Part II is a region-by-region examination of the length of the west coast from a paddler's perspective. Each region is discussed in a separate chapter, which begins with a regional outline and then spotlights what we feel are the choicest sea kayaking areas within the region. A total of twenty such areas are discussed. Each area description contains a map (*which is not to be used for navigation*), a data page and a narrative. The twenty areas include a broad range of sea kayak touring alternatives, from calm water weekend trips suitable for paddlers with children, to month-long expeditions on the exposed coast that will challenge advanced sea kayakers. Many of the trips are suitable for paddlers with canoes. The two key-maps on the following pages indicate the location of each trip area.

While our experience on the coast has taught us much about the techniques of sea kayaking, coastal navigation and lightweight camping, and we often share this knowledge with the reader, this book does not purport to be a "how to" manual on any of those topics. Our focus instead is Canada's west coast and what it offers the sea kayaker. For a discussion of sea kayaking technique see: *Sea Kayaking: A Manual for Long-Distance Touring* by John Dowd, and *Sea Canoeing* by Derek Hutchinson. The absence of published information on the practical aspects of kayak sailing and kayak kiting has inspired us to comment on these subjects in Appendix A. The addresses of all government agencies, Indian bands, conservation groups and transportation companies mentioned in the text, are contained in Appendix B.

In this book we use two different units of measurement to describe distances. Distances within each of the twenty trip areas are expressed in nautical miles, as this is the unit of measurement used in most nautical charts. Thus, wherever the term "mile" appears in this book, it refers to the nautical mile rather than the statute mile. All other measurements in the book are expressed in the metric system. One nautical mile equals 1.15 statute miles or 1.85 kilometres. One kilometre equals 0.62 of a statute mile. One metre equals 3.28 feet.

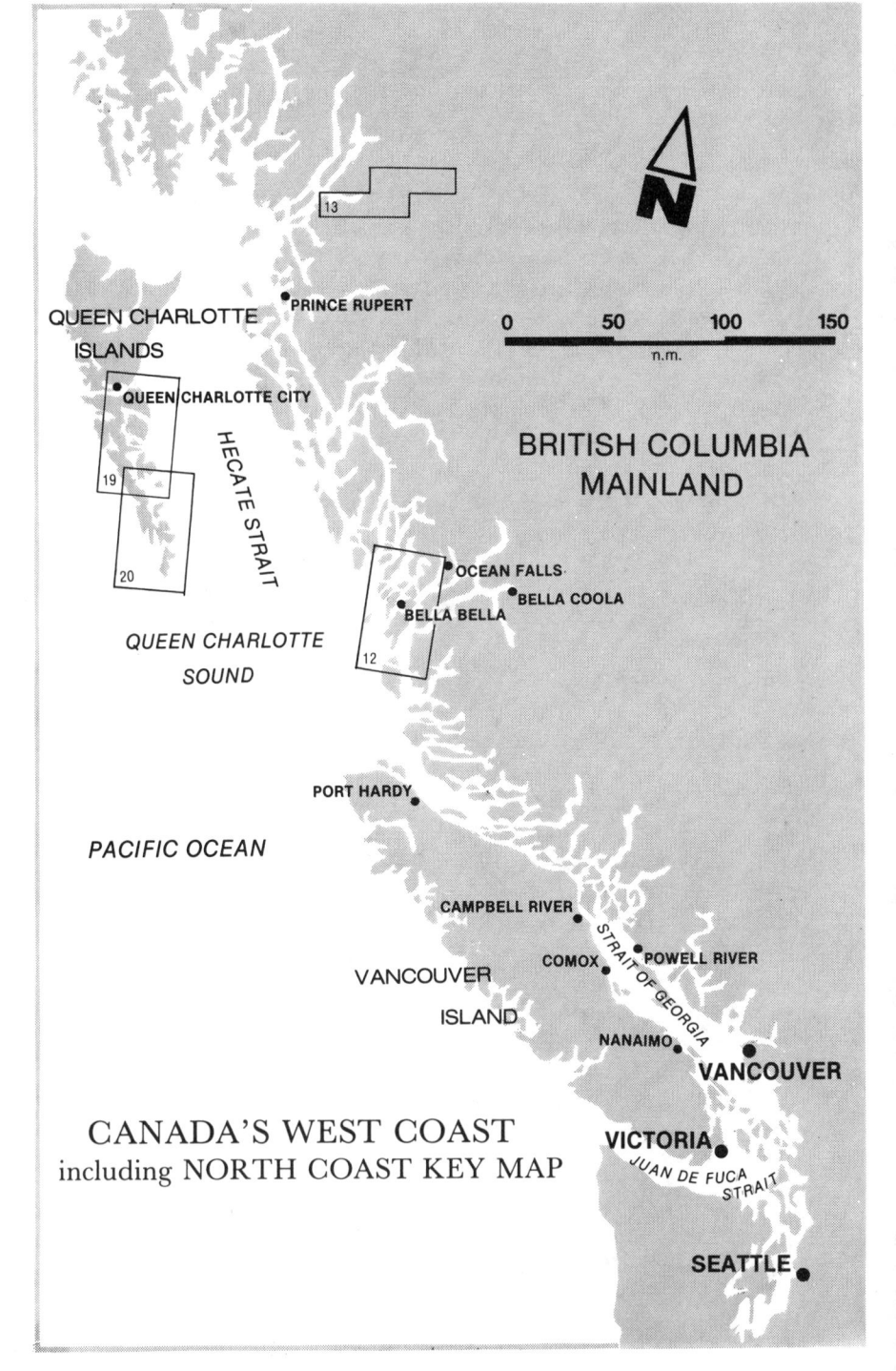

CANADA'S WEST COAST
including NORTH COAST KEY MAP

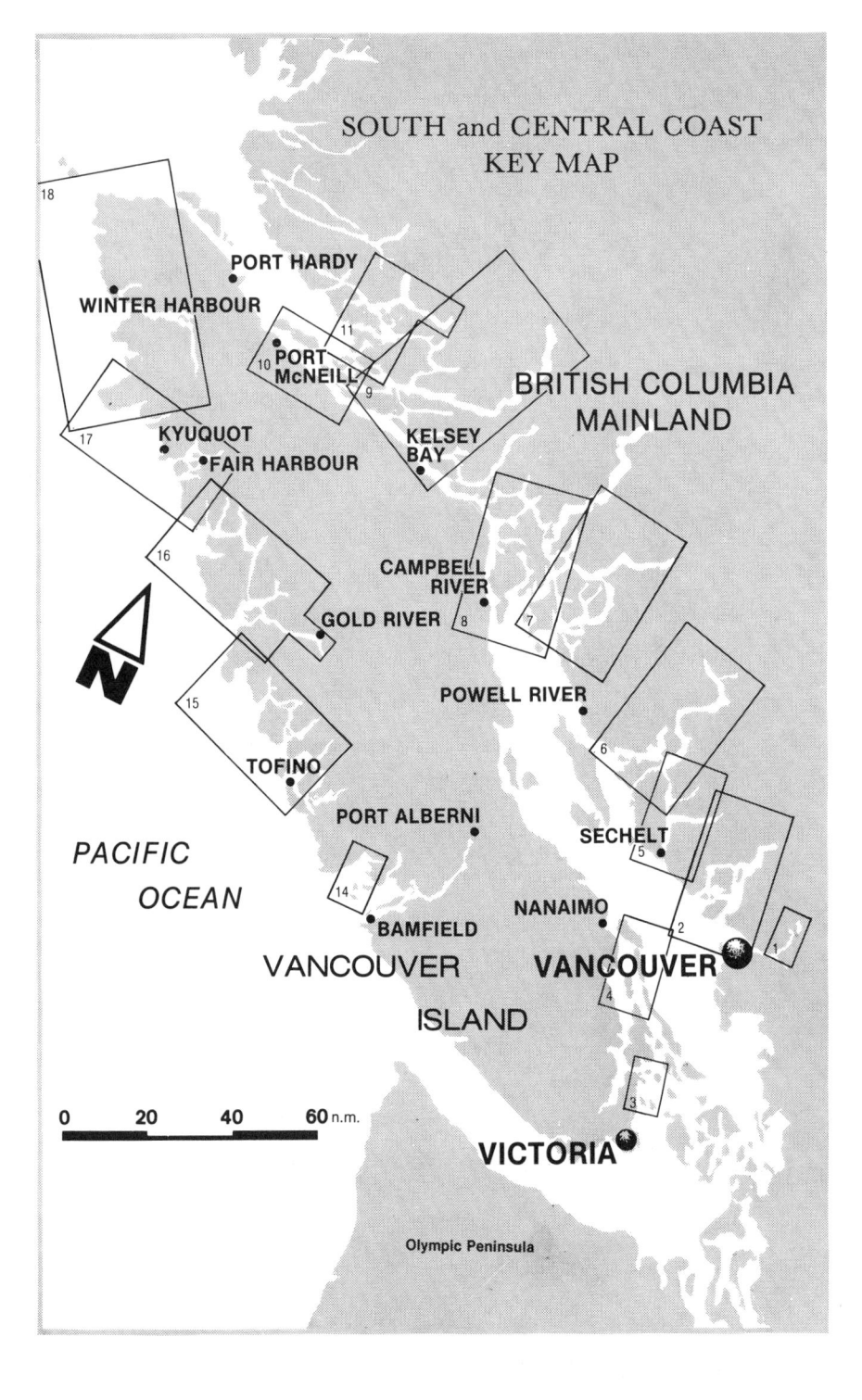

SOUTH and CENTRAL COAST
KEY MAP

PORT HARDY

WINTER HARBOUR

11

10 PORT
McNEILL

9

BRITISH COLUMBIA
MAINLAND

KYUQUOT

17

FAIR HARBOUR

KELSEY
BAY

16

CAMPBELL
RIVER

GOLD RIVER

8

7

POWELL RIVER

N

15

6

TOFINO

PACIFIC
OCEAN

PORT ALBERNI

SECHELT

5

14

BAMFIELD

NANAIMO

2

1

VANCOUVER

VANCOUVER

4

ISLAND

18

3

0   20   40   60 n.m.

VICTORIA

Olympic Peninsula

PART I

Chapter One
THE WEST COAST PADDLING ENVIRONMENT

Weather

The most popular kayaking season on Canada's Pacific coast is from June to August, when the weather is driest and mildest. Only the winter months, however, are unsuitable for most kayak touring enthusiasts. Our earliest trip was in March and our latest in November. A non-summer kayak trip risks inhospitable weather but offers compensating advantages: less boat traffic and more seclusion in the wilderness. The crisp air promotes visibility, and the coastal mountains look their best when tinselled with rain-fed waterfalls and draped in snow.

The coast's reputation for rain is well-known but often exaggerated. Although some weeks the rain never seemed to stop, we estimate that overall it rained only fifteen per cent of the time we were paddling. In the summer months it is not unusual to cruise for weeks under sunny skies.

To the kayaker, wind is the most important aspect of the weather. Wind affects the turbulence of the sea and the progress of a trip. The paddler should be familiar with both prevailing and cyclonic wind patterns in the trip area before setting off. Wind frequency diagrams for numerous places on the coast are published by the Canadian Hydrographic Service in the *British Columbia Small Craft Guide* (two volumes) and the *Sailing Directions* (two volumes). Weather forecasts which indicate wind direction and velocity are broadcast by the Canadian Coast Guard over various frequencies and/or VHF channels from eight stations on the coast: Vancouver, Victoria, Tofino, Comox, Alert Bay, Bull Harbour, Prince Rupert and Sandspit. If the kayaker does not have the electronic gear to receive these broadcasts, most fishermen and yachtsmen are happy to pass on the latest weather information, or, before launching the kayak, telephone the closest Coast Guard station for the current marine weather report. In the canyon-like inlets the mountainous topography makes wind forecasting especially difficult. The winds follow the zigzag of the inlets, flowing predominantly inland in the summer and the reverse in the winter. The frequency of inflowing and outflowing winds is approximately equal in the spring and fall. The mountainous topography is also responsible for gravity winds which can arise suddenly and build dangerous waves. Caused by cold highland air spilling out of the mountains onto the sea, these winds, called *Squamishes*, are common in inlets or along a coastline adjacent to a valley.

When traversing an unprotected coastline paddlers often travel in the early morning or evening, when winds are usually, though not always, negligible.

The fog veil

The Sea

The kayaker soon discovers that west coast waters are cold. The temperature of the sea averages between 5°C and 15°C (41°F to 59°F), though local conditions may create warmer or colder waters. It does not take long for a person to suffer hypothermia if immersed in such chilly seas, even in the summer. It is thus imperative that coastal paddlers be able to efficiently execute self-rescue or group-rescue procedures and be able to recognize and treat hypothermia.

The tides are the great engines of the sea. Caused mainly by the gravitational force of the moon, the rise and fall of the tides follow a predictable pattern throughout the lunar cycle. The tides with the greatest rise and fall, called spring tides, occur when the moon is full or new. Tides with the minimum range, known as neap tides, occur when the moon is in the first or third quarter.

The rise and fall of the water level is important to the kayaker mainly while ashore, because it affects the location of the kayaker's camp and the resting spot of the boat. Tide tables give the height and time of the daily high and low tides at a designated reference port which is usually the surrounding area's marine center. The tide tables also list the tidal differences in both time and height between a large number of secondary ports and the reference port. There is usually either a secondary port or reference port close enough to the kayaker's position to make tidal prediction relatively accurate. Issued annually by the Canadian Hydrographic Service and available at marine supply stores, two tide table booklets cover the Canadian Pacific coast: Juan de Fuca and Georgia Strait in one booklet and the rest of the coast in the other. The time indicated in the tide tables refers to Pacific Standard Time. Add an hour during Pacific Daylight Saving Time.

The tides create currents in the water. The velocity of tidal currents is a function of the rise and fall of the tides. As the tides follow a predictable pattern throughout the lunar cycle, so does the velocity of the tidal currents. Thus, during spring tides the tidal currents are strongest, and during neap tides currents are weakest.

As tidal currents have an important bearing on the progress of a kayak cruise, the paddler must determine their direction. We have met some novice kayakers who could not predict the direction of tidal currents, because they did not understand the basic principle that ebbing tides flow out to the ocean and flooding tides flow inland. In the south coast area Vancouver Island divides the tidal flow around its northern and southern extremities. The ebb tides divide and the flood tides meet near the northern end of Georgia Strait. Marine charts sometimes indicate the velocity and direction of tidal currents, a feathered arrow indicating the flood tide and a featherless arrow representing the ebb tide.

Generally speaking, the direction of a current changes around the time of high water and low water. So that mariners do not have to rely on this rough rule, the tide table booklets include current tables for designated reference and secondary current stations. The stations are usually located at passages where marine traffic is heavy and the tidal current is swift. The current tables indicate the time when the current turns direction, which is a short period known as slack tide. The table also indicates the time of maximum flow and the current's rate. The times are given in Pacific Standard Time.

There are virtually no waters along the coast that are off-limits to a capable sea kayaker. However, there are a number of hazards of which paddlers must be aware. At numerous locations the tide runs so swiftly that the water resembles a frothy mountain river. You need white water kayaking skills to navigate these passages successfully, except at slack tide when the waters are still. Thus, where a marine chart indicates that a waterway has a high velocity current (six knots or more) or where the chart designates whirlpools or rapids, the area should only be traversed at slack tide. Standing waves and overfalls, caused mainly by opposing winds and tidal currents, can also be a hazard to the paddler. These are common at the mouth of a river or inlet, especially when outflowing waters meet an inflowing wind. The sea off a headland is often choppy and confused.

Leaving the protected inside waters and paddling the exposed coast, the kayaker must deal with another oceanographic variable: swell. Bobbing up and down in deep swell and watching fellow paddlers disappear and then emerge again can be an unsettling experience to the novice and can even cause sea sickness. But swell is only hazardous when it breaks, either as a result of winds or opposing tidal currents or over a shoal, reef or beach. Staying upright in breaking seas taxes the paddler's stabilizing technique. Landing through surf with a fully loaded boat is not recommended. Surf is something to play in when your gear is safely ashore. There are very

Riding the waves

few places on the exposed coast where it is impossible to avoid the big breakers. A surfless landing spot sheltered behind an island, reef or spit can usually be found.

The marine traffic on coastal waters is often more worrisome than the sea itself. Skippers of fishing boats, tugs and pleasure craft will generally steer clear or throttle down if they spot a paddler. The onus is on the paddler to be seen.

Before travelling on the sea be sure to advise a friend or relative as to your paddling destination and the duration of the journey. If you fail to arrive when expected, the friend or relative can contact the Canadian Coast Guard and a search may be organized.

Flora and Fauna

A naturalist will be inspired by the west coast wilderness. It is teeming with life. The highly manoeuvrable sea kayak is easily the best craft in which to investigate this abundance. A basic knowledge of the plants and animals of the coast is not only aesthetically pleasing, it is also practical. Your safety or even survival may depend on it. The British Columbia Provincial Museum in Victoria publishes an inexpensive and informative series of natural history guides. Individual handbooks deal with the following subjects of interest to coastal paddlers: shore birds, waterfowl, mammals, ferns, grasses, mosses, mushrooms, barnacles, intertidal univalves, intertidal bivalves, seaweeds, marine fish, freshwater fish and foodplants of coastal native peoples. Also available from the Provincial Museum are two large maps which indicate the sea bird colonies of the Queen Charlotte Islands and Vancouver Island. Kayakers must take special care not to disturb nesting places at sea bird colonies.

Government reserves protect many of the coast's ecologically significant areas. For further information regarding the location of these sites, the habitat protected and the regulations which apply to visitors, contact the Ecological Reserves Unit in Victoria.

Some kayakers carry little "city food" when they paddle the coast, choosing to live off the sea. It is certainly possible to do this, but unless you want to make food gathering the focus of a trip, forget it. While seafood easily complements any meal, to rely on it for your daily calorie intake is an onerous chore. After a long paddle, the tired and hungry kayaker is often in no mood to spend further energy to catch fish, search for abalone or dig for clams. It is much easier to open a bag and pull out dinner. On the other hand, any kayaker who does not frequently enjoy the fruits of the sea is missing one of the very best attractions of a west coast paddling trip. Unfortunately, the coast is frequently visited by the red tide which contaminates many delicious species of shellfish, notably oysters, clams and mussels which feed on the red tide's toxic micro-organisms. Local offices of the Department of Fisheries and Oceans will advise which areas have been affected. Official warnings err on the side of caution and this has prompted many shellfish epicures to ignore them. This can be a deadly practice. Numbness in the lips is said to be the first sign that contaminated material has been consumed.

19

Belly-flop

The west coast is one of the last areas of the world where big undersea creatures abound. We have encountered grey whales, orca (killer) whales, sea lions and basking sharks. Even at close quarters we have never been disturbed by these powerful animals, though they might return any demonstration of disrespect. More bothersome are the black bears and wolves which frequently roam the seashore in remote areas on Vancouver Island and the mainland. Grizzly bears may be encountered in the isolated mainland inlets, especially near river estuaries. A kayaker must store food away from camp.

Cultural Environment

A kayak tour on the coast offers more than a wilderness experience. At isolated cabins, industrial camps or outpost communities the paddler meets the people who live on the coast, and at abandoned native villages, overgrown logging camps, mines, old canneries and whaling stations the paddler connects with the history of their forefathers. For a superb photographic study of the people of the coast, see *Coast of Many Faces* by Ulli Steltzer and Catherine Kerr.

The native people who inhabited Canada's Pacific coast created one of the richest pre-industrial cultures the world has known. Since the days of Captain Cook native Indians have had to cope with uninvited visitors. Kayakers are the most recent intruders and must see themselves in this light if problems are to be avoided. Most of the interesting Indian sites, both ancient and modern, are on Indian reserves. Such reserves are clearly marked on federal and provincial government topographical maps. Nautical charts frequently fail to designate them. The reserves are private property and should be respected as such. Before visiting a reserve obtain the permission of the band council which administers it. A letter to an Indian band sometimes inspires a reply, but telephone communication is usually more successful. Better still is to attend at the council office and receive personal authorization to visit native sites. On occasion we have had to convince suspicious band managers that we were not like other boaters who have defaced or stolen Indian antiquities.

The location of the most important Indian sites on the coast are well-known and of public record and hence we indicate their location in this book. In our travels we have discovered Indian burial caves, totem poles and rock carvings that have escaped public knowledge. To ensure their preservation we indicate only the general area where they can be found. Local native peoples usually know the precise location and may reveal this to an inquiring kayaker. Keep your hands and feet off all carvings, house timbers and skeletal remains.

One of the major attractions of the coast for touring paddlers is the scarcity of private ownership of coastal lands. Even where waterfront property is privately owned, private property ends at the high water line. The foreshore is public land and free for campers to use, except in the rare case where the government has issued shellfish harvesting and other leases.

A skull meeting

Environmental Protection

The vast scale of modern resource extraction threatens the special character of many of the best sea kayaking regions on the coast. Clearcut logging that denudes an entire watershed, and strip mining that carries away a mountainside, simply ruin an area for sea kayakers. We recognize that sea kayakers have no greater claim on the wilderness than loggers or miners. Conflicting interests must be balanced, yet so often the scales are tipped in favour of the loudest voice. Industry can afford expensive public relations campaigns. Nature cannot. Many of the environmentally sensitive areas on the coast will only be preserved if seen and enjoyed by greater numbers of people, a process that we hope this book will promote. We recognize, however, that such people may threaten the very environment sought to be protected. To prevent the overuse of specific camping spots, none are designated in this book, except those in provincial or federal parks. We hope that all paddlers will practice no-trace camping. Burn or carry out every piece of garbage. Keep your toilet away from streams and springs and bury it. Burn toilet paper. If kayak campers follow these basic rules, the west coast wilderness will remain a treasure.

Chapter Two
EQUIPMENT

To be safe and comfortable in the west coast environment the paddler must be properly outfitted. Even a weekend trip requires a surprising amount of gear. A checklist is indispensable in assuring that no equipment is forgotten. Many of the items included in the following checklist are optional.

Checklist and Notes

Boat gear

☐ boat
☐ paddle(s)
☐ spare paddle
☐ spray skirt
☐ repair kit
☐ boat slings

☐ bailer or pump
☐ sponge
☐ flotation bags
☐ sailing gear
☐ kite

Boat: The kayak — the people's yacht — is the most affordable of all cruising vessels, costing about the same as a colour television set. There are many types of kayaks on the market. Choosing a boat that suits your interests, experience and budget can be a difficult task. You must weigh and balance a number of conflicting factors. The most important of these are: a) number of seats b) stability c) durability d) transportability e) stowage space f) comfort g) price.

Repair kit and spares: It is easy to damage a boat and paddle on a coastal cruise. Reefs, surf and long stretches of rocky shoreline inevitably take their toll. On our trips we have snapped a number of paddles, broken a backrest and split our kayak's coaming. Spare

Equipment

Packed for cruising

paddles and a repair kit are essential items even on an overnight trip. A repair kit must contain the material to mend punctures in the hull, flotation bags or sponsons and, if the kayak is of the folding variety, damage to the frame. An inventory of spare screws, fastenings and fittings and a small fibreglass kit are invaluable. If your kayak has wire rudder or skeg cables, carry spare stainless steel cable. The minimum tools required are a screwdriver (preferably with a number of detachable heads) and pliers. Clamps are very useful too. Keep the repair kit in a waterproof container.

Boat slings: Frequently we have had to carry our boat distances equivalent to a city block or two over sand flats, shoreline hills and portage routes. On occasion the kayak had to be raised or lowered from a ferry and other vessels. Moving a fully loaded boat in and out of the water can be strenuous exercise. Boat slings made of seatbelt webbing or other material make these tasks easier. A length of the material can be slipped under each end of the boat and four persons can handily transport the craft. The slings should be long enough (at least five metres) to allow each person to pass the webbing over the shoulder, thereby distributing the weight evenly over the body. A solo paddler we encountered carried cylindrical plastic boat fenders and used these to roll his boat even over rocky shores.

Bailer or pump: If your kayak is not equipped with a built-in pump you must carry a bailer or pump. The latter is preferable as you can expel cockpit water with the spray skirt closed.

Sailing gear and kite: See Appendix A.

Carrying boat with slings

Equipment

A chart tablecloth

Navigational gear

- ☐ chart(s)
- ☐ tide and current tables
- ☐ watch
- ☐ compass
- ☐ dividers
- ☐ binoculars

Charts: The Canadian Hydrographic Service publishes nautical charts of Canada's western coastline. They are sold at marine supply and map stores. Chart 1 is a detailed legend which will assist the kayaker in translating the hundreds of symbols and abbreviations used on the nautical charts. The Canadian Hydrographic Service also publishes tidal current charts which indicate the direction and velocity of tidal currents in each hour of the tidal cycle at a few of the locations on the coast. Though nautical charts are easily the most useful maps for kayakers, topographic maps published by the federal and provincial governments are an asset especially if you want to explore the land behind the shoreline.

Virtually useless when wet, charts must be protected from the water. There are two methods. Charts can be carried in a waterproof plastic pouch, or they can be coated with liquid plastic or clear wall covering. We found the latter alternative preferable for a variety of reasons. Coated charts are generally easier to use and carry than charts that must be kept in a pouch. A coated chart is extremely durable and has many uses: as a miniature sail, tablecloth or cockpit covering. To minimize bulk and expense two charts can be fitted back to back, or single charts can be folded. Before applying the plastic coat, cut the appropriate tide and current tables and glue them to the chart. Trim the chart, but be sure to leave a portion of the vertical border intact as it will indicate a minute of latitude, which equals one nautical mile. If the compass rose is to be cut away, note on the chart the angle of declination. Coated charts should not be folded, as creases break the plastic. Roll them.

Watch: Essential for predicting tides and currents.

Compass: Every west coast kayaker should carry a compass and know how to use it on the water. There is no other way to navigate in fog, which is persistent in many parts of the coast in the summer.

Weather interpreting equipment

☐ barometer or altimeter   ☐ weather radio

Altimeter: An altimeter is a barometer which indicates changes in atmospheric pressure.

Weather radio: Economical pocket-sized VHF receivers are available on the market which can receive weather radio reports.

Safety gear

☐ life jacket   ☐ two-way radio
☐ wet suit or survival suit   ☐ flares
☐ survival kit   ☐ first aid kit
☐ tow rope   ☐ collapsible radar reflector

27

Equipment

Life jacket: Federal government regulations require that each paddler carry an approved personal flotation device.

Survival suits: Considering the cold temperatures of coastal waters, kayakers must consider carefully the various cold water survival systems. Immersion suits are available, though bulky and expensive, which can prolong life in the water for many hours. Unless your expedition is exceedingly daring, such as crossing Hecate Strait to the Queen Charlotte Islands, the likelihood of losing the kayak and having to use such gear is remote. More probable is a capsize where you will spend up to half an hour in the water before righting the kayak and climbing aboard. This is long enough for you to become dangerously chilled. If you are wearing a wet suit in such a situation, the chances of survival are very high. If there is any reasonable probability of capsizing, wear a wet suit. Farmer John/Jane style wet suits, made of ⅛" to ¼" neoprene, which leave the arms exposed, and which do not interfere with your ability to paddle, are ideal. Under normal conditions we do not wear our wet suits, trusting our experience and boat to keep our bodies out of the water. But if we have a long crossing to make, or we are venturing into heavy seas, we will don the neoprene. Wet suits are also worn in calm seas, if the weather is very cold and wet. They are functional at camp as well. Spread on top of a sleeping mat they make a rocky bed comfortable.

Survival kit: In exposed or very isolated areas of the coast, we paddle with a nylon moneybelt containing vitamins, fire starter, waterproof matches, a knife, and a mix of nuts and dried fruits strapped to our body. Such a pouch saved a couple who lost their boat and everything in it on the west side of the Queen Charlotte Islands.

Two-way radio: As there is frequent boat and plane traffic along most stretches of the coast, we have trusted flares or smoke signals to attract attention in the event of a disaster, such as the loss of a boat or a serious physical injury. However, in the isolated areas of the Queen Charlotte Islands and the north coast, electronic communication equipment is a worthwhile investment for the security-conscious paddler. Compact transceiver units with varying capabilities are available on the market, but these can equal or exceed the cost of the boat.

First aid kit: No sensible person explores the wilderness without a first aid kit. The degree of sophistication of the kit varies according to the individual preparing it. At a minimum, the first aid kit should contain the necessary pills, creams and bandages to treat the ailments which a west coast paddler may suffer: sea sickness, sunburn, cuts and gashes. An antiseptic is essential. One kayaker we met carried guarana tablets in his kit. Available at herb stores, they have an effect similar to a half dozen coffees and are useful when an emergency requires sustained energy.

Clothing

- □ 1 heavy sweater
- □ 1 light sweater
- □ windbreaker
- □ vest
- □ shirts
- □ 2 pairs of pants
- □ longjohns

- □ underwear
- □ shorts
- □ socks (including 1 woolen pair)
- □ footwear
- □ wool hat or toque
- □ gloves or mittens

Clothing - General: Wool and synthetic pile are the most popular clothing materials for the coastal climate as they provide warmth even when wet. Unfortunately, pile and wool take a long time to dry and mildew easily, though one expensive nylon product, Helly Hansen, dries amazingly quickly. For those on a tighter budget, try the summer trousers issued to letter carriers by the Canada Post Office. Lightweight yet warm, they dry in minutes. They are sold in surplus stores. Longjohns, mittens, a toque and a heavy sweater earn their passage even in the summer.

Footwear: A kayaker's feet are in the water every time the boat is launched or landed. In the summer, when wet feet are tolerable, many kayakers wear wet suit boots, sneakers or plastic (drip-dry) shoes. Such footwear is lightweight, easily packed and is comfortable to wear around camp. When paddling during the cold weather months it is essential to keep your feet dry. Rubber boots will do the job, but only in shallow waters. Even small waves can spill water into the boots. Hip waders offer the best protection. They are also an asset when foraging for shellfish or when loading a floating kayak. Always bring an extra pair of footwear suitable for long walks or hikes.

Equipment

Wet weather gear

- □ rain jacket
- □ rain pants
- □ rain hat
- □ rubber gloves or pogies

Breathable rain gear: For the past few years breathable rain fabric has been all the rage with the outdoor crowd. Along with other kayakers we have discovered that while the fabric definitely does breathe, it can also leak. Maybe the salt crystals from the sea foul the system. We have seen too many soggy paddlers wearing this product. Beware. The level of exercise and the coast's rainy-day temperatures are low enough to prevent mugginess when wearing non-breathable rain gear.

Rain jacket: The fewer the seams, the better. All seams must be sealed. The sleeves should be fitted with elastic or velcro cuffs to prevent water dripping down the arm.

Two cruising perspectives

Rain pants: Essential if you want to move about a rainy camp. Lightweight rain pants are adequate.

Rain hat: Get one that keeps the rain off your face. With rain slanting into your eyes, it is very difficult to navigate. A sou'wester is perfect, but a hood over a sun visor or baseball cap will do.

Rubber gloves or pogies: A kayaker's gloves must permit a firm grip of the paddle and should keep water off not only the hands but also off the wrist and lower arm. Gauntlet style mechanic's gloves or pogies are recommended. Pogies are mittens designed specially for paddlers. They cover the hands yet permit the bare fingers and palm to wrap around the paddle shaft.

Personal gear

☐ day pack
☐ pocket knife
☐ toiletries
☐ toilet paper
☐ towel
☐ spare prescription glasses with safety cord or contact lenses
☐ needle and thread
☐ sunglasses with safety cord, or sun visor
☐ sun hat
☐ sun cream and/or sun screen

☐ lipsalve
☐ insect repellant
☐ personal medication
☐ notebook and pencil
☐ book(s)
☐ game(s) and/or musical instruments
☐ pee bottle
☐ water bottle
☐ alarm clock
☐ surfing helmet

Alarm clock: It is often necessary to depart early in the morning to take advantage of favourable weather, wind or tide. An alarm clock assists pre-dawn departures.

Surfing helmet: For a person who wants to play in the breakers.

Sleeping gear

☐ tent with fly, or tarp and bivy bag
☐ sleeping bag

☐ sleeping pad
☐ netting

Equipment

Tent: In the summer months many people kayak the coast without tents, preferring bivy bags and a tarp. Bugs are a problem in certain areas. Only tents or bivy bags with no-see-um netting can guarantee an itchless sleep.

Sleeping bag: On all our trips we have used down-filled sleeping bags, but these are not really suited to the humidity of the coastal climate. They can be perpetually clammy. Bags filled with synthetic material, though more bulky, are preferable. They absorb very little moisture. If such bags get wet they still provide warmth and dry quickly.

Cooking gear

☐ stove
☐ fuel
☐ matches
☐ lighter
☐ spare lighter
☐ fire starter
☐ water container(s)

☐ frying pan
☐ pot(s)
☐ potholder
☐ can opener
☐ cup
☐ eating implements
☐ tin foil

Fires: There is no shortage of firewood on the coast, although finding dry wood is sometimes difficult. A piece of cedar is usually available which, when split open, is fine fuel. Fire starter is another alternative. We always carry a small stove for use when weather conditions or our laziness thwart a fire.

Water container: Though rivers and streams are rarely difficult to find on the coast, the best camp spots are often far from fresh water. The kayaker must be able to store drinking water. The water container that we use is not designed for water at all, but wine. Some Canadian wineries sell their product in a foil-coated plastic bag which is fitted with a spout. The six-litre bag is surprisingly durable, collapses to nothing when empty, and when filled can be shaped to fit a free space in the boat.

Eating implements: These are easily lost. A friend solved this problem by cutting a hole in the handle of a spoon and in the rim of an eating bowl, and connecting the two by a long piece of codline.

32

Film cannister spice box

Camping gear

□ plastic tarp
□ flashlight or headlamp
□ spare batteries
□ candles
□ hatchet

□ folding saw
□ collapsible shovel
□ nylon cord(s)
□ sharpening stone

Plastic tarp: A sheet of plastic has many uses in a kayaker's camp. It can cover the cockpit of the boat in the rain and can shelter food, gear and people. Or make a sauna with it. Drape the plastic over a dome-shaped frame of saplings and seal the assembly with rocks or sand. In a bonfire roast a dozen large stones. Do not use sedimentary or river rocks as they burst easily. Carry the red hot stones with a flat piece of driftwood and deposit them in a pit centered in the dome. Spill fresh water (not salt water) over the rocks and enjoy the steam bath.

Equipment

Fishing gear

☐ handline or collapsible rod
☐ lures
☐ trolling weight
☐ landing net or gaff
☐ gutting knife

☐ crab and/or prawn
   traps with line
☐ collection bag
☐ fishing licence(s)

Doggie for dinner

Landing net or gaff: Landing a salmon in a kayak is almost impossible without a landing net or gaff.

Traps: Crab is abundant on many stretches of the coast and in a few areas there are prawns. For the latter, you need a trap with at least 100 metres of line. To mark the position of the trap in the water, retrieve a brightly-coloured float from the beach and tie it to the line.

Collection bag: Cod is the foodfish most easily caught on the coast. The spiky spine of a rock cod can inflict painful wounds. Carry it in your kayak in a bag made of sturdy material.

Fishing licence(s): Required for both freshwater and saltwater fishermen. The freshwater fishing permit is issued by the British Columbia Fish and Wildlife Management, and the saltwater permit by the federal Department of Fisheries and Oceans. Both can be purchased at fishing supply stores. Along with the licences, be sure to get the free fishing guides for both tidal and non-tidal waters, published by the federal and provincial governments respectively. No licence is required to take shellfish, but the kayaker should be familiar with the daily catch limits, which are usually higher than any kayaker could reasonably consume.

Undersea monsters

Equipment

Diving or Snorkeling gear

☐ wet suit (including hood,   ☐ fins
   mittens and socks)   ☐ snorkel
☐ weights   ☐ collection net
☐ mask

General: A large number of west coast kayakers carry this bulky gear. It is not hard to understand why. Underwater enthusiasts rate Canada's Pacific coast as one of the best diving areas in the world. For detailed information about the coast's diving opportunities see *141 Dives in the Protected Waters of Washington and British Columbia* by Betty Pratt-Johnson.

Camera gear

☐ camera   ☐ lens paper and blow brush
☐ waterproof camera bag   ☐ film
☐ extra lenses

Waterproof camera: A sea kayaking cruise offers a vast range of subjects to explore through a lens: abstract natural patterns, photogenic kayaks, maritime wildlife, majestic scenery, happy faces. These subjects must often be recorded in conditions hazardous to both camera and kayaker. Countless times we have wanted to grab for a camera to capture scenes such as the sea in a squall or a fellow paddler riding the crest of a wave, but did not dare expose the vulnerable equipment to the elements. If you are serious about taking photos while at sea, acquire a waterproof camera. It can be slung around your neck, ready to shoot the action. We finally invested in a weatherproof Fujica 35 mm camera, and while the quality was inconsistent, the successful pictures justified the purchase. The Nikonos unit is superior but more costly.

Waterproof camera bags: A non-waterproof camera must be stored in a durable waterproof buoyant container, preferably with an opening that allows quick access to the gear. Durability is the most important factor in choosing a waterproof camera container.

Lenses: Sea lions, whales, birds and most other wildlife will elude a photographer who lacks a telephoto lens.

Blow brush: Salt crystals and sand on the lenses are inevitable on a west coast paddling trip. A blow brush is essential.

Packing gear

☐ duffle bag(s)   ☐ ziplock bags
☐ garbage bags (heavy duty)   ☐ stuff sacks

Duffle bags: If you must use public transport to get to the trip area it is advisable to collect all the gear into as few bags as possible. Large volume duffle bags are excellent for this purpose. They are also very useful around camp for storing food and for carrying gear to and from the boat.

Transporting Equipment

Most of the prime kayaking areas on the coast are accessible by public highways, logging roads or ferries. Some areas, however, can be reached conveniently only by plane. It is not difficult to transport a folding kayak by plane. Both Pacific Western Airlines and CPAir, which serve the major towns on the coast by jet, allow each passenger two free bags. The two heavy bags containing our folding boat have often inspired sharp words from baggage handlers: "What do you think this is — a freight train?" but neither airline has ever rejected the bags or imposed an excess baggage fee. The airlines will not allow a passenger to carry campstove fuel. Air BC, which provides scheduled float plane service to many small communities and lumber camps on the coast, charges excess baggage fees for luggage weighing over twenty kilograms. It is often cheaper for a group of kayakers to charter a float plane rather than use scheduled flights. Moreover, charter passengers have the convenience of being able to choose the time of departure. The De Havilland Beaver, the flying workhorse of the coast, can accommodate four kayakers, two double-seater collapsible boats and enough gear for a two to three-week trip. The De Havilland Single Otter can transport at least six people, three double-seater collapsible kayaks and enough gear for a two to three-week trip.

Equipment

Three methods of transport . . .

Very few planes can accommodate a rigid kayak. It is possible to fly these boats on the pontoons of a float plane. The vast majority of float plane operaters on the coast do not provide this service as they lack the special insurance coverage and mounting fittings which are required if external loads are to be carried. Rigid kayaks can be shipped to various remote locations on the coast via Coast Ferries Ltd., a Vancouver-based freighter service.

PART II

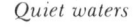

Quiet waters

Chapter Three
GREATER VANCOUVER

Vancouver is the main gateway to Canada's west coast. There is much here to interest sea paddlers. Numerous shops sell and rent kayaks, canoes and paddling accessories. Vancouver has an active sea touring kayak club. Two commercial outfitters offer guided kayak touring expeditions. The Museum of Anthropology at the University of British Columbia features a superb collection of Indian artifacts and totem poles, many of which were removed from abandoned Indian villages discussed later in this book. The Vancouver Aquarium is a fine introduction to the marine life encountered by the coastal paddler. Finally, the Main Branch of the Vancouver Public Library has a well-stocked clipping file and a special Pacific Northwest book collection which can provide valuable information about a proposed trip area.

Vancouver has many day trip paddling options including English Bay, False Creek, the Vancouver Harbour (beware of the treacherous tide rips at First and Second Narrows), and the Fraser River estuary. An excellent guide to the latter is *Explore the Fraser Estuary!* by Peggy Ward. Experienced sea kayakers who enjoy exertion should consider the most adventurous day trip in the region: a crossing of Georgia Strait. The crossing between the Tsawwassen ferry terminal and Galiano Island is twelve miles. Over twice that distance is the route between Nanaimo and Vancouver. The direction of the winds on the day of the journey should determine the direction of the crossing.

The two areas discussed in the following pages are just a half-hour drive from Vancouver's downtown skyscrapers. Yet each offers a taste of the wilderness to the paddler who is willing to venture for more than a day. The protected, usually calm waters are ideal for those who want to develop kayak touring skills. Both trips are suitable for family excursions.

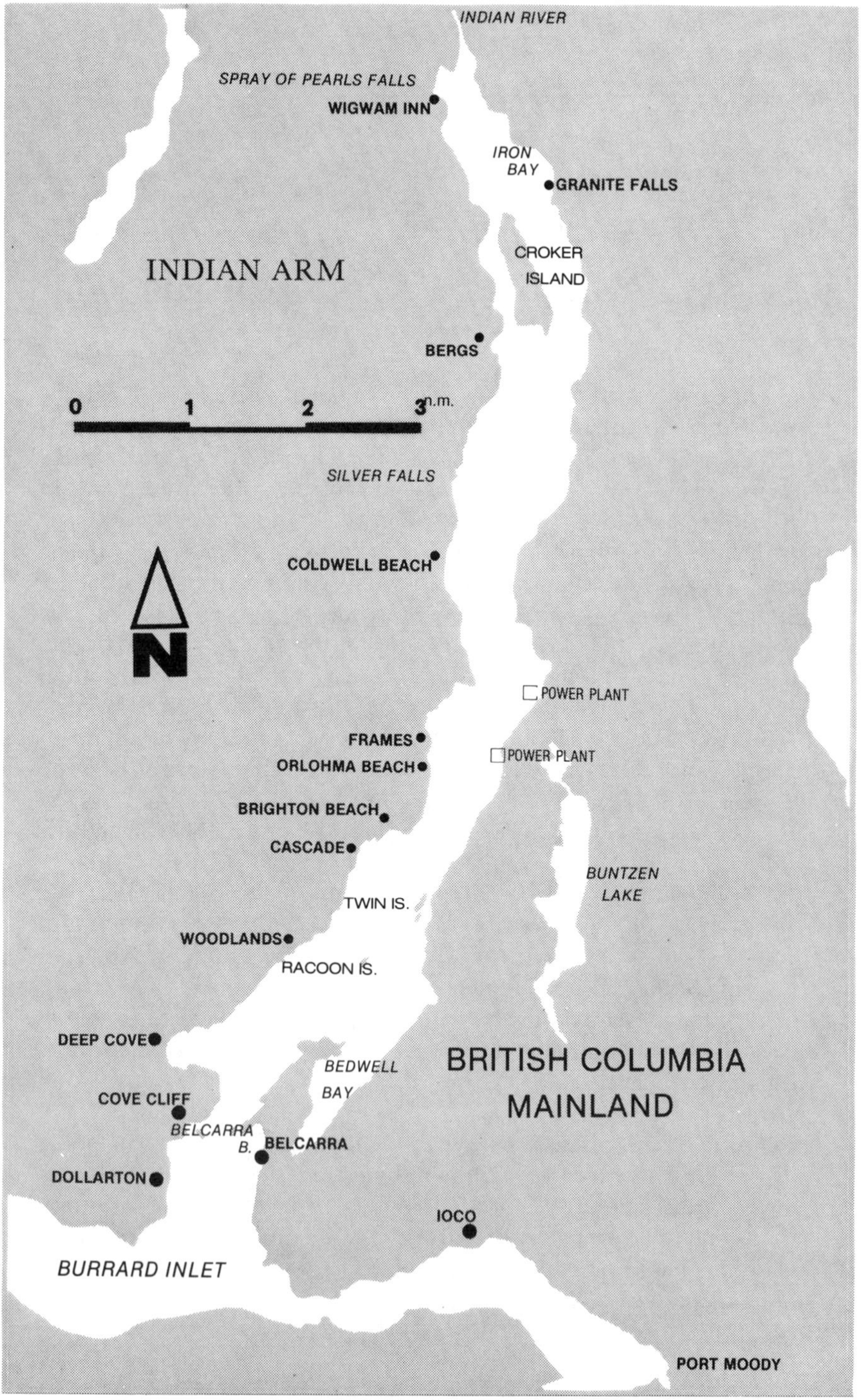

INDIAN RIVER

SPRAY OF PEARLS FALLS
WIGWAM INN●

IRON
BAY
●GRANITE FALLS

CROKER
ISLAND

INDIAN ARM

BERGS●

0   1   2   3 n.m.

SILVER FALLS

COLDWELL BEACH●

N

POWER PLANT

FRAMES●
ORLOHMA BEACH●

POWER PLANT

BRIGHTON BEACH●

CASCADE●

BUNTZEN
LAKE

TWIN IS.

WOODLANDS●

RACOON IS.

DEEP COVE●

BEDWELL
BAY

BRITISH COLUMBIA
MAINLAND

COVE CLIFF●

BELCARRA
B.
BELCARRA

DOLLARTON●

IOCO●

BURRARD INLET

PORT MOODY

Indian Arm

Area 1

Attractions: Minutes from Vancouver. Typical coastal inlet: fine mountain scenery, waterfalls, islands, river estuary, logging camps. The north end of Indian Arm is only 10 miles from civilization, yet you feel isolated.

Access: Launch at the south end of Indian Arm, either on the east side at Deep Cove or on the west side at Belcarra Bay. Deep Cove is 9 km east of the Second Narrows Bridge in North Vancouver. Drive north over the bridge and follow the signs to Deep Cove. Belcarra Bay is 28 km east of Vancouver. Follow Hastings Street and the Barnet Highway to Port Moody. From Port Moody follow the signs to Ioco and then on to Belcarra. Plenty of parking at both launching spots.

Seascape: Protected waters, usually calm. Perfect for beginners and families.

Hazards: Much small boat traffic. Be conspicuous. Watch for boat wakes.

Season: March to November. Least congested and most scenic in early spring and fall. Indian Arm receives over double Vancouver's precipitation, mainly in the winter.

Length: 2 to 4 days.

Camping: The Twin Islands near the south end of the Arm are within a park and camping is permitted. Some of the beaches along the southern half of the arm are unsuitable for camping due to the close proximity to cottages. Abandoned logging or quarry sites are best.

Chart: 3495 Vancouver Harbour Eastern Portion,
          Indian Arm Inset   1:30,000

Introduction

Protected Indian Arm is an excellent place for a maiden voyage. It is perfect for a weekend trip, though you could easily linger a few days longer. It offers a chance to leave civilization behind without travelling far.

Burrard Inlet to Buntzen Power Plant

Vessels of every description furrow the waters around Deep Cove, Belcarra Bay and Bedwell Bay. It is best to take the wakes head-on or off the bow's quarter. Dress colourfully or fly a flag and thereby minimize the chance of a collision. Heading north you will soon pass Racoon Island and the Twin Islands. They constitute the Indian Arm Islands Marine Park. There are a few spots to pitch a tent on the Twin Islands but bring water. There is a spring on the north Twin Island but it is difficult to find. On the west side of the Arm roads end at the tiny community of Woodlands and houses begin to peter out as you paddle north . . . until they return again clustered near the beaches at Cascade, Brighton Beach, Orlohma Beach and Frames. Heading north, the two grey stone powerhouses of the Lake Buntzen power complex (one started its service in 1914) speak of a by-gone era and contrast sharply with the plush suburban architecture further south. At the Lake Buntzen power plant stretch your legs. Stroll up to the lake, a 20-minute walk.

Buntzen Power Plant to Indian River

North of Coldwell Beach there are few cabins on either side of the Arm. From the Lake Buntzen power plant north, along the east side of the Arm, a power line cuts a wide unsightly swath, but the visual impact is mitigated by the stream-gushing mountains which rise abruptly from the water's edge to heights exceeding 1000 metres. On the west side of the Arm many fine stretches of shoreline cliffs are pastelled with lichen. North of the pretty Silver Falls are the remains of a mining operation which the forest is reclaiming. Steepsided Croker Island is the home for eagles, gulls and herons, and is usually ringed with log booms.

Granite Falls is a highlight on this trip. The multi-tiered falls are spectacular and the surrounding area is full of surprises: a bouncy suspension bridge, rusting mill equipment, ancient trucks and tumbled buildings. Just north of the river a trail leads up to what must once have been a picnic site. From this spot there are fine views over Iron Bay to the head of the Arm. Granite Falls has always attracted visitors. Before the turn of the century, the Union Steamship Company scheduled regular Sunday excursions here. Litter is the depressing sign that Granite Falls is still popular. Across the Arm some crumbling wharfs protrude from the shoreline, creating geometrical silhouettes on the horizon.

Wigwam Inn, near the north end of Indian Arm, has a very colourful history. Built in 1910 as a luxury resort by a German entrepreneur and visited by such notables as John D. Rockefeller, rumours circulated that it housed subversives of the Kaiser. The fortunes of the Inn have plummeted and soared through the decades. The RCMP once raided the place, searching for an illegal gambling operation. After years of neglect the Inn has recently been refurbished in the grand style of its early days. Dinner visitors are welcomed. A trail leads behind the Inn up to the spectacular Spray of Pearls Falls.

Wigwam Inn

47

"It won't start!"

The kayak is a fine vantage point from which to observe British Columbia's number one industry in action — at the logging operation across the inlet from Wigwam Inn. Trucks straining under a load of timber roar down from the mountains. An immense A-frame crane lifts the logs and dumps them into the water, creating a minor tidal wave. The crane lifts the trailer of the truck onto the cab, piggy-back style, and the outfit returns to the hills. A little tugboat, its bow toothy like the jaw of a shark, pushes the logs into a boom. Lots to see here.

At high tide you can paddle a short distance up the Indian River. Snags, rotting piles and mud flats at the mouth of the river can obstruct the passage. Fine fishing though. Near the mouth of the river we had an interesting social experience. We came upon a small boat which seemed to sprout fishing rods. A group of six people, including a wee child and an old toothless gentleman, was jigging for cod. Each person tugged a line. Their little craft had dangerously little freeboard and we were surprised that they had ventured so far. But they had known far more perilous sea voyages: in the South China Sea. They were Vietnamese refugees, "boat people." In broken English they told us that they regularly travelled up Indian Arm to "take free food."

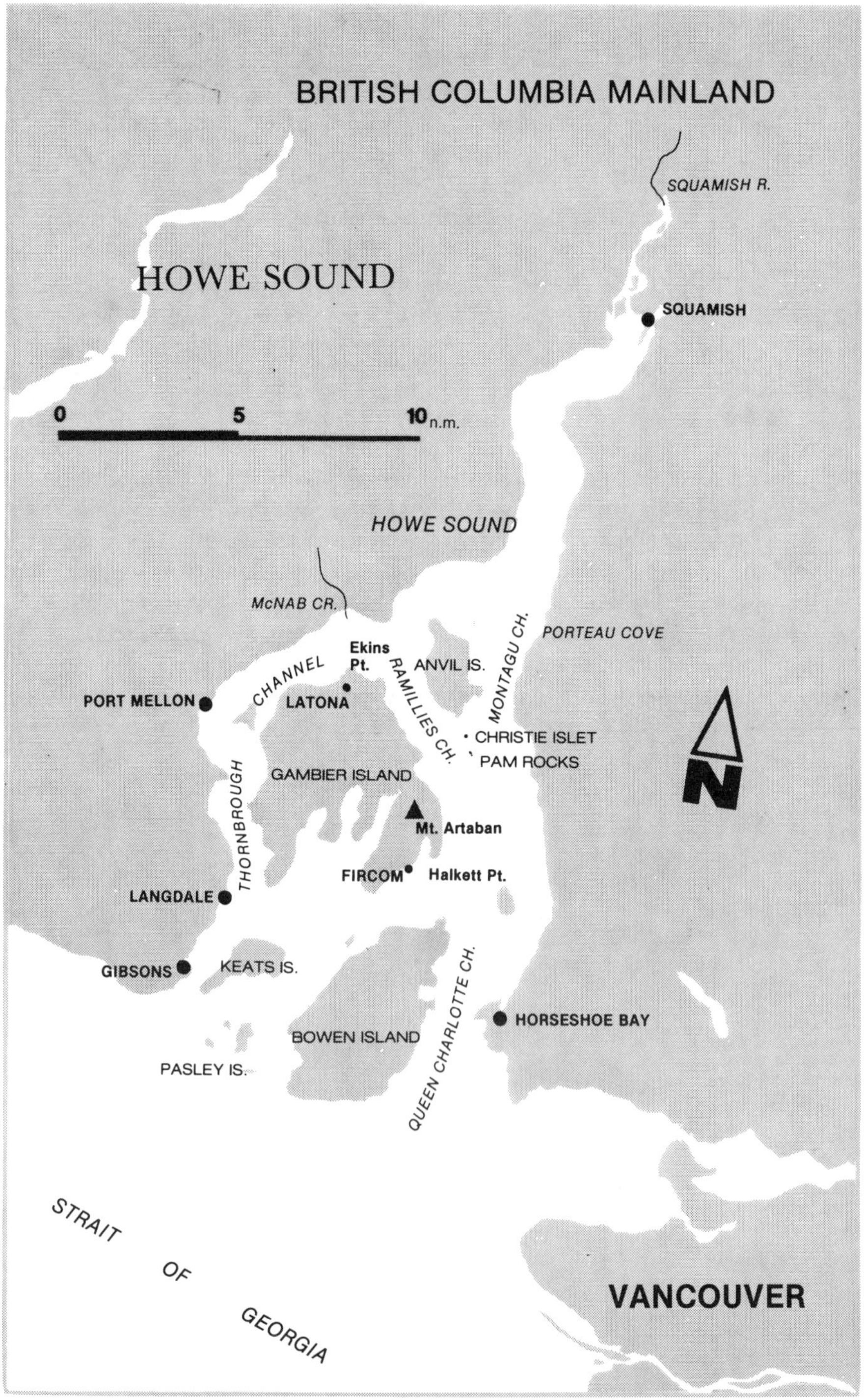
BRITISH COLUMBIA MAINLAND
SQUAMISH R.
HOWE SOUND
SQUAMISH
0
5
10 n.m.
HOWE SOUND
McNAB CR.
PORTEAU COVE
MONTAGU CH.
Ekins Pt.
ANVIL IS.
RAMILLIES CH.
CHANNEL
PORT MELLON
LATONA
CHRISTIE ISLET
PAM ROCKS
N
THORNBROUGH
GAMBIER ISLAND
Mt. Artaban
FIRCOM
Halkett Pt.
LANGDALE
GIBSONS
KEATS IS.
QUEEN CHARLOTTE CH.
HORSESHOE BAY
BOWEN ISLAND
PASLEY IS.
STRAIT OF GEORGIA
VANCOUVER

Howe Sound

Area 2

Attractions: Spectacular mountains overlooking the sound: from the nearby Lions to the distant Garibaldi peaks. Good fishing. Bird sanctuary. Seal colony. Island hiking. Close to Vancouver.

Access: Launch at Porteau Cove on the east side of Howe Sound or across the sound at Port Mellon. Porteau Cove is 25 km north of the Horseshoe Bay ferry terminal on Highway 99. To get to Port Mellon take the car ferry from Horseshoe Bay to Langdale. Leaving the Langdale ferry terminal, turn right and drive 11 km north to Port Mellon.

Seascape: Mostly protected. Short crossings between the islands.

Hazards: Avoid Queen Charlotte Channel as boat and ferry traffic is heavy. Occasionally a strong wind, called a *Squamish*, which blows south out of the mountains, can whip up dangerous seas.

Season: March to November. Least crowded and most scenic in the early spring and fall.

Length: 2 to 4 days.

Camping: Fine beaches and potable stream water on Gambier Island.

Chart: 3526 Howe Sound   1:40,000

Introduction

Howe Sound is interesting sea kayaking territory, even though it is difficult to find the wilderness here, as bustling civilization is so close at hand. The northern half of the sound is clearly preferable, as the islands south of Gambier Island (Bowen, Keats, Pasley) offer very few camping opportunities away from cabins and roads. Queen Charlotte Channel is a marine turnpike. As the mainland periphery of the northern half of the sound is bordered with power lines, a highway and railroad, the best sea kayaking is along the unspoiled coastline of Gambier and Anvil Islands. The northeast coast of Gambier Island has a few exceptional sand or pebble beaches. Incredibly, a mining company is seriously proposing that a huge chunk of Gambier Island be mined. A citizens' committee is resisting these plans. Gambier Island can be circumnavigated easily in two days. Allow another day to explore Anvil Island.

If you launch at Porteau Cove you will cross Montagu Channel, which is often choppy due to local winds which can be funnelled to significant velocities by adjacent mountain walls. Port Mellon, the other recommended launching spot, is on the protected

East coast Gambier Island

Thornborough Channel, where the water is usually calm. If you launch at Seaside Park, just north of the Port Mellon pulpmill complex, ask the receptionist at the mill for permission to park your vehicle there.

Thornbrough Channel

The fishing on the northern side of the channel is excellent. McNab Creek empties out of a sweeping valley onto a kilometre long beach that invites a jogger. A logging camp is situated on one end of the beach and some cabins cluster at the other. An Indian pictograph just east of the creek is hard to find: ask local residents for precise directions. Howe Sound has the heaviest concentration of log booms in the world. You will find many on Thornbrough Channel, hugging the vertical shores of Gambier Island. Log booms are dangerous. Keep off.

From Ekins Point, at the northern tip of Gambier Island, an old logging road leads behind the Thunderbird Yacht Club and Latona Youth Camp up to Gambier Lake. Do not miss this hike. The return trip takes only 1½ hours. Your legs and lungs will get a work-out in an aromatic second growth forest. The lake, set in a natural bowl, will be warm if any sun has been shining, and may yield a trout or two. Fantastic echoes here.

Ramillies Channel

This is the finest sea kayaking area in the sound, allowing the paddler to forget the reminders of industrialism which fringe the mainland. The Gambier side has some fine beaches which afford good views up and down the sound. Across the channel, the cliffs on aptly-named Anvil Island are most impressive, especially when tinted scarlet in the setting sun. Anvil Island offers very few camping spots. Cabins overlook the beaches on the east side of the island. The best overnight spots are where least expected, on the flat ledges above the rocky shoreline.

Christie Islet, directly south of Anvil Island, is a sanctuary for a noisy congregation of gulls and cormorants. Watch out for aerial bombardment. Do not go ashore as it could cause nest desertion. Further south, a seal colony inhabits the Pam Rocks. Resting on the rocks just above the waterline, the seals flop into the water at the approach of a boat.

After the paddle . . .

South Gambier Island

On a chart, the five peninsulas of south Gambier Island look like crippled fingers. Cabins dot the coastline of each of the peninsulas and the bays between are often crowded with log booms and recreational boats. Old logging roads fan north from these bays and make for interesting hikes. Just west of the fine bluffs at Halkett Point a trail leads from the wharf at the United Church's Fircom Camp up to Mt. Artaban. Allow four hours for the hike to the top and back.

An incident on one of our trips to Howe Sound shows how important it is to carry a compass even when kayaking familiar waters. We were heading south from Gambier Island to Gibsons, across the Langdale-Horseshoe Bay ferry lanes when the low-lying clouds descended right to the water. Visibility was reduced to a boat length. We heard a ferry blast and decided to dash back to Gambier. But where was Gambier? A quick compass reading and a frantic paddle took us out of harm's way.

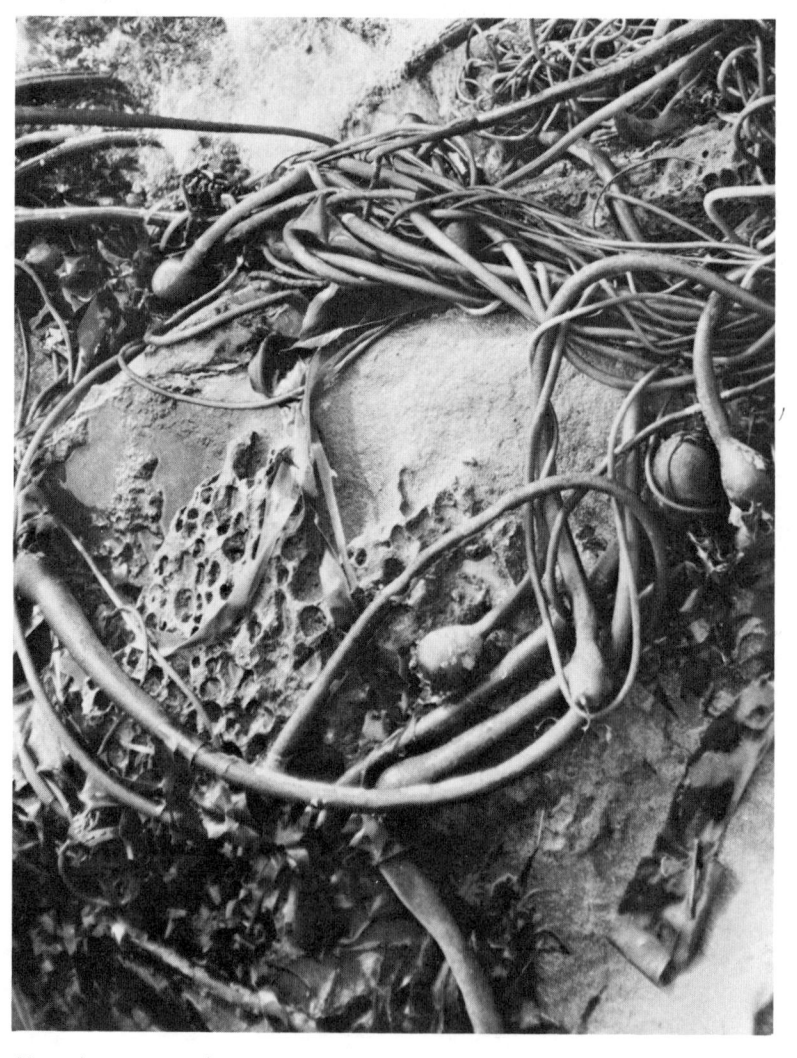

Nature's ornamentation

Chapter Four
GULF ISLANDS

Situated mid-way between the cities of Vancouver and Victoria is a group of islands which comprise one of the most popular cruising areas in the world: the Gulf Islands. In a word, these islands have personality: rustic old farms and funky artistic communities, derelict trawlers and shiny inboard pleasure craft, thick evergreens and satin-smooth arbutus, seals and sea bird colonies. The annual precipitation is lower than anywhere else on the coast. No wonder that the islands are rapidly being developed, especially those with paved roads and ferry service.

Virtually anywhere in the Gulf Islands is suitable for sea kayaking. The waters are mostly protected, but there are numerous inter-island crossings which require some experience and confidence. The major drawback of the Gulf Islands for touring paddlers is the lack of shoreline camping sites. The coastline here has few beaches; it is mostly jagged rock. Most of the waterfront, even on the small islands, is privately owned. "No trespassing" signs abound. While this does not really interfere with daytripping it can be a real hassle for expedition paddlers.

The two areas discussed in the following pages are the best in the Gulf Islands for multi-day trips. They provide a sample of everything the Gulf Islands have to offer.

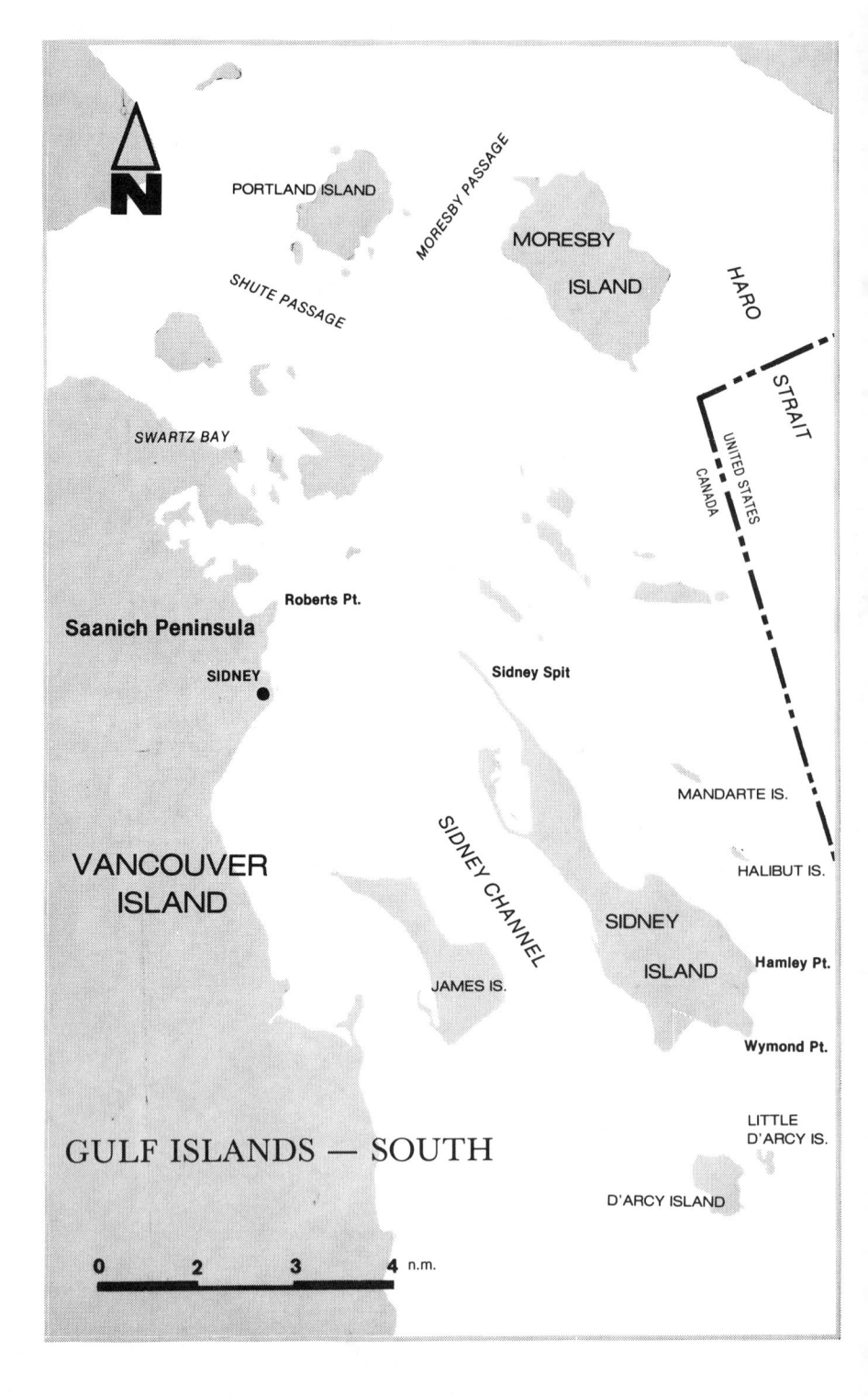

N

PORTLAND ISLAND

MORESBY PASSAGE

MORESBY

ISLAND

HARO

SHUTE PASSAGE

STRAIT

UNITED STATES

CANADA

SWARTZ BAY

Roberts Pt.

Saanich Peninsula

SIDNEY

Sidney Spit

MANDARTE IS.

HALIBUT IS.

**VANCOUVER
ISLAND**

SIDNEY CHANNEL

SIDNEY

ISLAND

Hamley Pt.

JAMES IS.

Wymond Pt.

LITTLE
D'ARCY IS.

GULF ISLANDS — SOUTH

D'ARCY ISLAND

0   2   3   4 n.m.

Gulf Islands — South

Area 3

Attractions: Three island parks, each a naturalist's paradise. Seafood smorgasbord. Island hikes. Close to Victoria.

Access: By car. Launch at Sidney, 26 km north of Victoria on Highway 17. Put-in either south of the town at the beach near the Anacortes ferry terminal or just north of the town at Roberts Point, which is accessible via residential streets. To reach Sidney from Vancouver take the ferry from Tsawwassen to Swartz Bay and drive 5 km south on Highway 17.

Seascape: Both protected and open waters. A number of crossings are longer than a mile.

Hazards: Much small boat traffic between Swartz Bay and Sidney. Stay clear of the busy ferry terminal at Swartz Bay.

Season: March to November. Flowers best April to June. Congested on summer weekends. Perfect mid-week trip.

Length: 2 to 5 days.

Camping: With three parks, no problem.

Chart: 3441 Haro Strait, Boundary Pass
and Satellite Channel   1:40,000

Gulf Islands

Introduction

The natural history of the islands off the northeast coast of the Saanich Peninsula is so exceptionally rich that it is easy to forget that suburbia is just a few miles away. D'Arcy Island, Portland Island and a large part of Sidney Island have been preserved as parks. Each island has an intriguing past. The mild, frequently sunny weather, the many sand beaches, the abundant seafood, and the hints of history combine to give this area a distinctly Mediterranean character.

Sidney is a bustling town with all the facilities a kayaker requires. Of the launching sites, Roberts Point is preferable as your parked car is safer there than at the more open beach south of Sidney. Do not forget to load up with drinking water before leaving as it is scarce on the islands. The ideal route is a circuit down to D'Arcy Island, up to Sidney Spit, over and around Moresby Island, across to Portland Island and then back to Sidney, or in the reverse direction, depending on the tides. Begin south on the circuit when the tide is ebbing, or north if flooding. The tidal current here is significant. At a leisurely pace, the circuit takes four to five days. Shorter trips can focus on particular islands.

Sidney to D'Arcy Island

Sidney Channel ushers the paddler south to James Island. "No trespassing" signs are conspicuous on the island, and for good reason. World War II ammunition was manufactured on James Island and it is still used as an explosives depot. With the pastoral scenery you would never know it. You will probably find earnest salmon fishermen off the southeast coast of James Island. It is a "hot spot." The south end of the island looks as if it has been hacked off by a giant cleaver. It rises abruptly in broom-covered cliffs. Across the channel the sand cliffs bordering the west coast of Sidney Island are equally impressive.

D'Arcy Island, now a park, once had unusual residents. From 1892 to 1924 it was the home for a colony of lepers, mainly oriental immigrants. D'Arcy Island is a gem. There are numerous fine beaches for camping. It affords scenic views across Haro Strait to the San Juan Islands in the United States, and down the length of the Saanich Peninsula. It abounds with deer and otter, and a group of seals lazes about the rocks in the passage between D'Arcy Island and

D'Arcy Island

Little D'Arcy Island. An overgrown trail rings the island and takes the hiker over pebble beaches, meadows, rocky promenades and through a dense forest. The flora is exceptionally rich, a botanist's dream. Allow three hours for the walk.

Sidney Island

Except for its northern tip, Sidney Island is privately owned. Cliffs make most of the island inaccessible to kayakers. The southern end of the island looks like ranch land — lots of open space between the trees. No rain forests here. Two beautiful beaches curve between Wymond Point and Hamley Point, but almost every shoreside tree offensively proclaims "No trespassing." Remember that private property ends at the high water line. In the middle of Sidney Island is a private aircraft landing strip which doubles as a pasture.

Offshore, Halibut Island was once inhabited and is reported to have a freshwater spring. Mandarte Island, a barren slab further north, is one of the most important bird colonies on the coast. Look for glaucous-winged gulls, pelagic and double-crested cormorants and pigeon guillemots. Even tufted puffins have been spotted here.

Gulf Islands

The marine park at the north end of Sidney Island is designed for crowds with a dozen picnic tables, a large wharf and numerous mooring buoys. You will also find water and toilets. The park is busy from mid-June to mid-September. We were the only visitors on a mid-week trip in May. Probably the best camping is on the beach on the east side of the spit, just south of the piles. Here are fine views of the offshore islands and few reminders that you are in a developed park. The intertidal zone offshore is crammed with delicious cockles and clams, which seem to thrive despite the numbers of spade-carrying visitors. The tasty bivalves are buried in the sand and are retrievable only at low tide.

A system of trails threads through the park leading to an open meadow. Rabbits, deer and even peacocks were introduced to the island years ago. We saw none of the latter but we met a few rabbits and a herd of deer. Grazing in the meadow, two dozen of the deer bounced into the bush upon our arrival. Not far from the meadow, close to the water, lie the remains of a brick mill, established in 1906. Sidney Island bricks form part of the stately Empress Hotel in Victoria. The mill closed during World War I.

Heron, Sidney Spit

Sidney Spit invites beachcombers. A variety of shore birds stroll along it, leaving trident tracks in the sand.

Moresby Island

From Sidney Island a four-mile crossing is necessary to reach Moresby Island. On a calm day the water can be as smooth as glass. Privately owned and having just a few good beaches, Moresby Island is not special. The attraction is the trip, not the destination.

Crossing over to the south end of Moresby, you are within a mile of the U.S. border. Haro Strait, bending around Stuart Island in the San Juan Islands at Turn Point, is a long stretch of open water. Haro Strait is an important shipping route and you can expect to cross paths with an ocean-going freighter. Kayaking across Haro Strait from the San Juan Islands, a friend almost died of fright when a monstrous black submarine broke the surface and then sank back into the depths.

Portland Island

In crossing Moresby Passage the tidal current is a factor. It moves as fast as three knots north on the flood, and south on the ebb. Portland Island is also known as Princess Margaret Marine Park, named in honour of Princess Margaret, who upon receiving the island as an official gift on a royal visit in 1958, donated the property to the people of British Columbia. The park is undeveloped. The island is the highlight of the trip. It has a number of fine beaches and the surrounding water is clear. It is criss-crossed with trails which are stamped down by wild sheep and deer. A trail cut by youth workers encircles the island and meanders along a shoreline cliff, through an abandoned farm (with pastures, orchard and stream), across a crushed-shell beach and over rocky bluffs covered with flowers. Idyllic. The island deserves a day or two.

Ferries rumble along both sides of Portland Island going to and from Swartz Bay. The swell produced is relatively harmless though it can cause surf on the shoreline and spill water into a kayak there. The route back to Sidney, across Shute Passage and through the islands off Swartz Bay can be extremely congested with small boats. Half a dozen large marinas are nearby. Be conspicuous.

GULF ISLANDS — NORTH

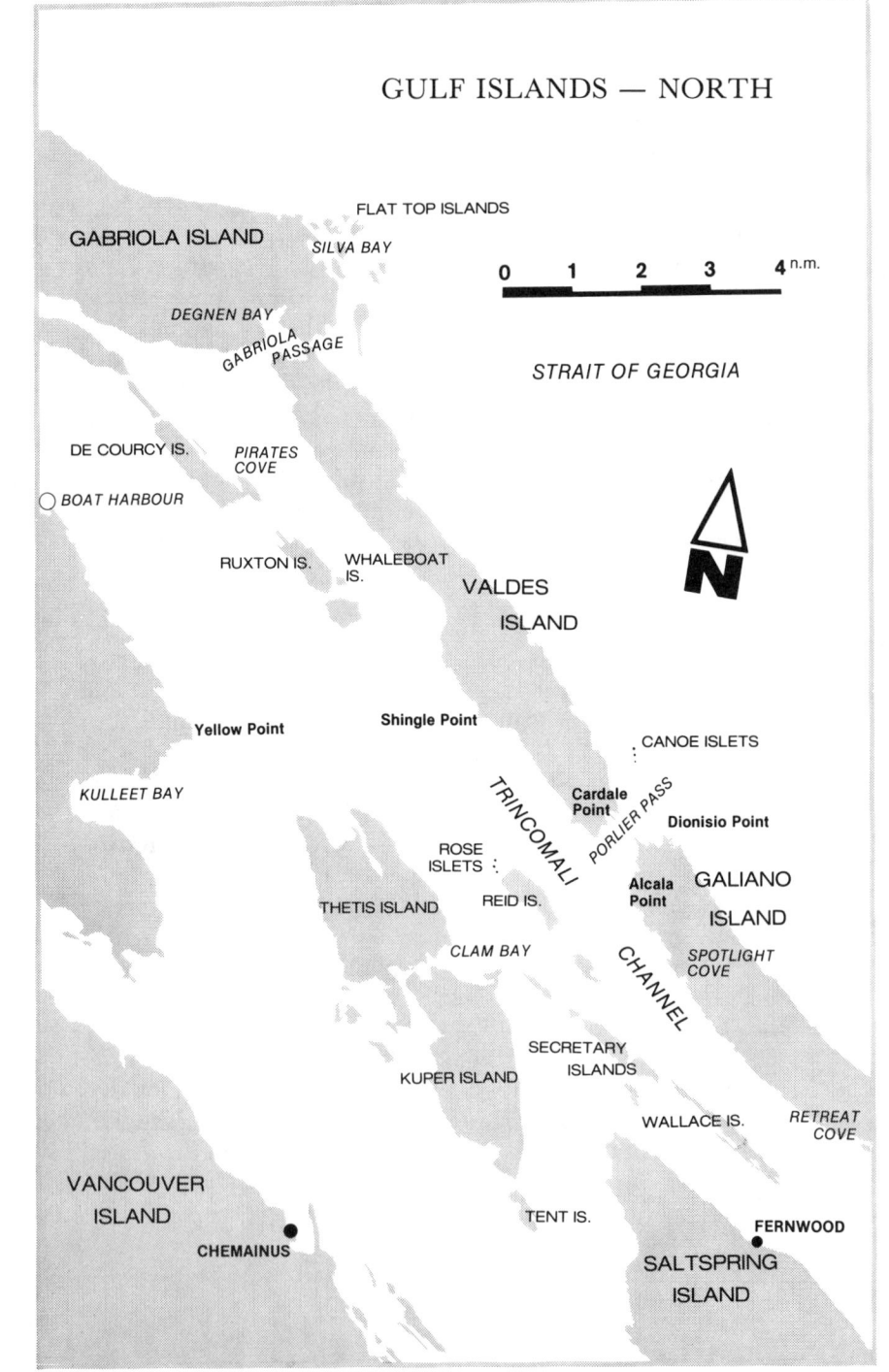

FLAT TOP ISLANDS

GABRIOLA ISLAND

SILVA BAY

DEGNEN BAY

GABRIOLA PASSAGE

STRAIT OF GEORGIA

0   1   2   3   4 n.m.

DE COURCY IS.

PIRATES COVE

○ BOAT HARBOUR

RUXTON IS.

WHALEBOAT IS.

VALDES

ISLAND

N

Yellow Point

Shingle Point

CANOE ISLETS

KULLEET BAY

TRINCOMALI

Cardale Point

PORLIER PASS

Dionisio Point

ROSE ISLETS

REID IS.

Alcala Point

GALIANO

THETIS ISLAND

ISLAND

CLAM BAY

SPOTLIGHT COVE

CHANNEL

SECRETARY ISLANDS

KUPER ISLAND

WALLACE IS.

RETREAT COVE

VANCOUVER

ISLAND

TENT IS.

FERNWOOD

CHEMAINUS

SALTSPRING

ISLAND

Gulf Islands — North

Area 4

Attractions: A coastline of cliffs and naturally sculptured rock. Indian petroglyphs. Island chains and clusters. Open waterways in which to increase your paddling confidence. Good fishing in the passages to Georgia Strait.

Access: On Vancouver Island launch from Yellow Point or Boat Harbour, which are between the towns of Nanaimo and Ladysmith. On Saltspring Island launch at Fernwood, north of Ganges. On Galiano launch at Retreat Cove. Both Saltspring and Galiano Island are connected by car ferry to Tsawwassen near Vancouver and Swartz Bay near Victoria. A small car ferry operates between Vesuvius on Saltspring Island and Crofton on Vancouver Island. On Gabriola Island launch at the south end, either at Silva Bay or Degnen Bay. Frequent ferry service connects Gabriola Island and Nanaimo. Another launching alternative is Thetis Island. A car ferry crosses to Thetis Island from Chemainus on Vancouver Island.

Seascape: Varied. Trincomali Channel: waters generally flat. One to two-mile crossings between the islands. Georgia Strait: open water paddling, frequently choppy. Porlier Pass and Gabriola Passage: swift tidal currents.

Hazards: Marine traffic, whirlpools and tide rips in Porlier Pass and Gabriola Passage.

Season: March to November.

Length: 2 to 7 days.

Camping: Difficult to find good camping spots. Beaches are scarce. Developed campsites at the provincial park at Pirates Cove on De Courcy Island. Camping is not permitted at Drumbeg Provincial Park at the south end of Gabriola Island.

Charts: 3442 North Pender Island to Thetis Island   1:40,000
       3452 Thetis Island to Nanaimo   1:40,000

Gulf Islands

Introduction

The area between the north end of Saltspring Island and the south end of Gabriola Island is an excellent place to enjoy the usually mild-mannered outdoors, yet still be challenged in the cockpit. The landscape bears little evidence of the presence of man; only a few cottages. The shoreline along the route is at once a barrier and an attraction. Most of the shore is craggy, beaches of sand or pebble are very rare, and landing and camping are difficult. On the other hand, much of the rocky shoreline deserves display in an art gallery: a set of fangs jutting out from an overhanging ledge; a perfect rock sphere ready to roll into the water at the kick of a giant's foot; acres of honeycombed sandstone. Nowhere else on the west coast did we find the sea's rim so fascinating, and because the land frequently rises abruptly out of the water, it is easy to cruise just an arm's length from shore and thereby inspect and photograph nature's ornamentation.

The tide currents in this area are significant. Even in the wide channels the currents can exceed three knots. In the passes, the currents can flow at nine knots during spring tides. The flood tide flows north through the channels and east out of the passes, the opposite with the ebb tide.

Getting to the recommended launching sites is half the fun of this trip as it involves a scenic ferry ride and a pleasant drive through the pastoral communities on the largest of the Gulf Islands. Stop at the craft workshops, the neighbourhood pubs or the local store and chat with the friendly islanders. For those launching at Retreat Cove on Galiano Island, consider a feast before or after the trip at the Pink Geranium, a few kilometres north. A more unusual location could not be imagined for a home-cooked gourmet restaurant that the guidebooks and patrons rate as the finest on the west coast of Canada. Reservations are recommended. The ferry from Tsawwassen to Galiano and Saltspring Island is one of the few on the west coast that will accept car reservations. Although standby chances are generally good, it is advisable to reserve weeks in advance.

Trincomali Channel

Launching from the government docks at Retreat Cove on Galiano Island or Fernwood on Saltspring Island, try to time the departure with the flood tide. About one mile north of Retreat Cove, the Galiano coast is a dramatic stretch of cliff, the longest we have seen

Sandstone gallery, east coast Galiano Island

on the coast. Milky stains on the cliff indicate a large concentration of birds. See especially the cormorant colony one mile south of Spotlight Cove. The birds will desert the lip-thick ledges with a tremendous flap at the approach of a paddler. At Alcala Point near the north end of the island the eroded shoreline pleases the eye.

Across Trincomali Channel, the string of rocks and islands from Wallace Island to Reid Island are populated with deer, seal, heron and otter, but few people. However, a best-selling author, David Conover, has a handsome house on one of the islands. His books *Sitting on a Saltspring, One Man's Island* and *Once upon an Island* have told the world about island life. The gull and cormorant habitat at the Rose Islets has been preserved as an ecological reserve.

Kuper Island is an Indian reserve. The mission was built in 1880. There is no need to describe the edibles at Clam Bay. The sandstone formations on Tent Island, south of Kuper, are notable. Across from Thetis Island, just south of Yellow Point on Vancouver Island is Kulleet Bay where many of the finest Indian petroglyphs on the coast are located. For further information consult *Indian Petroglyphs of the Pacific Northwest* by Beth and Ray Hill.

Gulf Islands

No ferry travels to Valdes Island, and that best explains why very few people have homes or cabins there. The entire east coast of the island, except for the spits at Cardale Point and Shingle Point, lack any landing potential. The cliffs are impressive though.

Camping sites have been developed at Pirates Cove Marine Park on De Courcy Island. Expect a crowd of boaters here on a holiday weekend or any time in the summer months. De Courcy Island has an exotic past. In the 1920's it was the refuge for a religious sect. The leader of the sect, known as Brother Twelve, claimed to be the earthly incarnation of a cosmic god and thousands of people took him seriously, sending trunkloads of cash. He disappeared in 1933, along with the loot. Rumours still persist that he left some behind, buried on De Courcy Island or on Valdes Island.

Tiny Whaleboat Island, off Ruxton Island, south of De Courcy is a provincial park.

Trincomali Channel

Gabriola Passage and Porlier Pass

The tide races through Gabriola Passage creating moderate tide rips and whirlpools. The currents here change 35 minutes before the change at Active Pass, which is referenced in the current tables. At Degnen Bay ask residents to point out the fine petroglyphs carved in the sandstone below an Indian midden. At Drumbeg Provincial Park (camping prohibited) we found what seemed to be a huge lump of jelly in a hollow in a rock near the waterline. Gentle probing produced the squirt and generalized slither of an octopus.

Silva Bay has a marina and a neighbourhood pub. If the much ballyhooed bridge across Georgia Strait is ever constructed, it is expected to ram Gabriola Island somewhere near here.

The Flat Top Islands are a salmon and cod fishing haven. The islands are private property and the owners are not friendly to campers, and for good reason. A negligent visitor let his campfire wander into the forest.

With the rocks, the traffic and the speed of the current, Porlier Pass deserves respect. The current tables indicate the time of slack water at Porlier Pass. There are two fine sand bays on either side of Dionisio Point. A decade ago dozens of squatters' shacks dotted the cove. The alternate community was so sizable that its food (organic, of course) was shipped in on a barge. Now it is the weekend hang-out of the recreational vehicle crowd. The Canoe Islets are an ecological reserve. Look for gulls and cormorants here.

The East Coast of Valdes and Galiano Island

This coast resembles the exposed coast of Vancouver Island in its unoccupied ruggedness. Looking across the open expanse of Georgia Strait to the city of Vancouver and the coastal mountains you feel far from the urban sprawl. On a clear day, snow-capped Mount Baker is spectacular. The waters here are often disturbed and usually tumble ashore. Landing the boat on this lonely coastline can be a challenge. But the shoreline rewards the visitor with mile after mile of exquisite sandstone sculptures, and in the driftwood which the rocks have captured, a creative eye can see a whale, a laughing face, a sailboat. The forest behind is a delightful blend of trees — pine, Garry oak, cedar and arbutus. The forest opens to the sea with rainbow-coloured mosses and lichen, tall grasses, Indian paintbrush, maybe even a rare dwarf cactus. Take it all home inside your camera.

Gulf Islands

You will see eagles along this coast. Unfortunately their numbers are decreasing, especially on Galiano Island, as more patches of the forest are logged. Perhaps due to that fact some of these creatures are hostile. One dove at us as we ate lunch at a small cove. It came so close we could see its talons. Even when we brandished our paddles it was not deterred. It swooped down again. Was this attack revenge for the recent loss of a tree-top home?

Eye spy   *Photo: David John Smith*

Chapter Five
SECHELT AREA

Just 50 km northwest of Vancouver, behind the oddly shaped Sechelt Peninsula, a series of inlets penetrate a mountainous wilderness of spectacular beauty. Though the scenery is the main attraction, there is much more to delight the paddler: Indian rock paintings, seafood, hinterland personalities, sea rapids.

The two areas discussed in the following pages comprise most of the sea kayaking territory east of the Sechelt Peninsula. West of the peninsula is Georgia Strait. The coastline here is fine for day paddlers but most touring kayakers will find it too close to homes, cottages, cabin-cruisers and runabouts. For weekend touring try the undeveloped coastline of Nelson Island which is just off the northern tip of Sechelt Peninsula. The basins and bays which poke into this coastline are miniatures of the inlets to the east.

A highlight of the Sechelt area is the Indian pictograph art on shoreline rocks. Most of the paintings are very difficult to find. We indicate their location as precisely as possible, but even with this information, be prepared for a hunt.

The Sechelt Peninsula is reached from the south by car ferry from Vancouver (Horseshoe Bay to Langdale) and from the north by car ferry from Powell River (Saltery Bay to Earls Cove). Highway 101 runs the length of the peninsula connecting the two ferry terminals.

TZOONIE RIVER

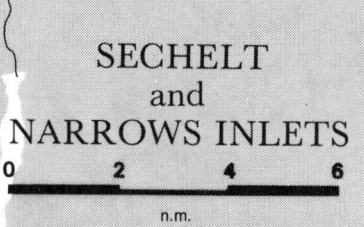

SECHELT
and
NARROWS INLETS

SKOOKUMCHUK
NARROWS

EGMONT

SECHELT RAPIDS

0   2   4   6

n.m.

NARROWS
INLET

TZOONIE NARROWS

SECHELT

STORM BAY

SALMON INLET

N

Kunechin Point

KUNECHIN ISLETS

HALFWAY ISLET

Nine Mile Point

Skaiakos Point

INLET

Tuwanek Point

Sechelt Peninsula

BRITISH COLUMBIA

LAMB ISLETS

MAINLAND

PORPOISE BAY   Porpoise Bay Park

SECHELT

STRAIT OF GEORGIA

GIBSONS

Sechelt and Narrows Inlets

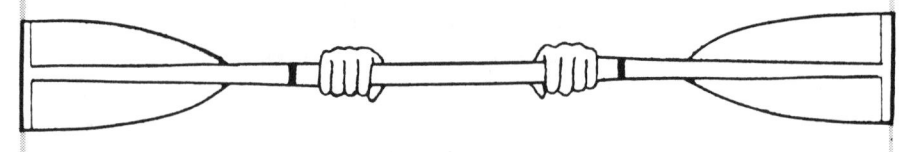

Area 5

Attractions: Sea gorges. Abundant shellfish (crab, oyster, clam). Tidal rapids. Easily accessible wilderness environment.

Access: From the town of Sechelt (28 km north of the Langdale ferry terminal on Highway 101) follow the signs to Porpoise Bay Provincial Park. Continue past the park turnoff and launch where the road comes close to the water, adjacent to some islands just south of Tuwanek Point.

Seascape: Protected inland waters. Usually calm.

Hazards: Watch for floating log debris. Extreme caution required at the northern end of Sechelt Inlet where the tidal flow of the Sechelt Rapids can reach 12 knots. Navigate only at slack tide.

Season: April to October. Enough territory here to avoid weekend boaters.

Length: 3 to 6 days.

Camping: Many fine beaches.

Chart: 3589 Jervis Inlet and Approaches   1:76,400

Sechelt Area

Introduction

Sechelt and Narrows Inlets are well-suited for kayakers who want a fjord cruise but who lack the experience and time for an extended paddle into the great inlets further north. An energetic paddler can travel from the launching spot to the head of Narrows Inlet and back in a long weekend. The recommended route avoids Salmon Inlet, the south arm of Sechelt Inlet, as it is heavily logged and slashed with power lines.

Launch at Tuwanek Point. The wilderness starts here. The coastline south of Tuwanek Point is a string of houses. Egmont, a village at the northern end of Sechelt Inlet is another launching alternative, but the paddler is immediately confronted with the Sechelt Rapids which can only be traversed at slack tide, and then only with extreme caution. The tidal currents throughout the rest of the area are moderate.

Sechelt Inlet

The well-designed homes which dot the Lamb Islets off Tuwanek Point are the pleasing end points of civilization. There are numerous beaches on both sides of Sechelt Inlet up the mouth of Salmon Inlet. The beaches at Tuwanek Point, Skaiakos Point, Nine Mile Point, Halfway Beach, Kunechin Point and Kunechin Islets have been designated as recreational areas by the provincial government. Camping is permitted. You will find chopped wood and pit toilets at the Tuwanek camping area. Look for a pictograph depicting a face on a cliff between Nine Mile Point and the creek one mile south.

The Kunechin Islets and Point provide fine views of the peaks which tower over Salmon Inlet. If you are an aviation fan you will enjoy this spot as it is the intersection of important float plane corridors. Every hour planes pass here en route to the many logging camps along the inlets. If the clouds are low the planes will buzz just above the surface of the water, like giant flies.

Sechelt Inlet is separated from Georgia Strait only by a flat isthmus of land where the town of Sechelt is located. Funnelled up the inlet, Georgia Strait winds can create choppy seas. We have had some wild rides in the white caps here. Another hazard is the floating logging debris. There is so much of it that local boaters have held public meetings to discuss the problem.

Storm Bay

Storm Bay is a treat. Once an active counter-culture community, it looks north up Sechelt Inlet to layers of mountain ranges. On the west side of the bay is a dainty group of islets, on the opposite side, a 400-metre cliff. At the end of the bay you will find an expansive intertidal area. Delicious oysters. Fringing the coastline are numerous cabins, including some fine driftwood creations. Much of the waterfront property is privately owned. The stream which empties into the bay flows through a hushed jungle of fir and fern. Here we discovered a rope swing, a thick nylon line dangling from the overhanging limb of an immense tree. Jumping from a hillside platform you swing out over the treetops, tasting an eagle's freedom.

An intimate connection with the great rhythms of nature is one of the charms of kayak touring. An incident at Storm Bay illustrates this well. We set up camp on the beach at a place we thought was above the high tide line. Awakened by the splash of water near the tent, we extended our hands outside. The waterline crept up our fingers, covered our hands and almost reached our wrists, but then slowly retreated. It was as if we had been greeted by another being.

Seaweed curtains

Near Tzoonie Narrows

Narrows Inlet

This pinched indentation in the mountains is one of the narrowest of all coastal inlets. There are a few logged patches here and there, but there are no vast clear-cut areas yet. Part of the north end of the inlet is scheduled to be logged by helicopter. A helicopter logging operation, though noisy, is fascinating to observe. The chopper flies up the mountainside and while hovering just above the treetops drops a cable to which a fallen timber is fastened. The aircraft lifts its heavy bounty clear off the ground, swings it down to the water and then releases it. Splash! This procedure is repeated every ninety seconds. A helicopter logging camp is portable. The floating hanger, landing pad and bunkhouse are situated atop a barge. After picking clean a patch on a hill, the rig is towed away.

Tzoonie Narrows, the most scenic spot in the inlet, is best paddled with the favourable tide. Tidal streams here can reach four knots. Remember that in all inlets the flood tides move into the inlet, the ebb tides move out. On the north side of the narrows the cliffs rise 1000 metres, ending in two immense knobs. A multitude of streams sluice down the inlet walls into waters where fishermen boasted of good cutthroat fishing. There are many stretches of gravel beach and no shortage of campsites in this inlet. The government has designated the beaches on each side of Tzoonie Narrows as recreational areas. Towards the end of the inlet are a few cabins, a bellowing waterfall and a logging camp that looks like a quaint village. At the head of the inlet, scattered rotting piles, a boggy shoreline and grassy flatlands mark the Tzoonie River estuary. The flatlands are tempting for camping but are invariably submerged at high tide.

Sechelt Inlet, under sail

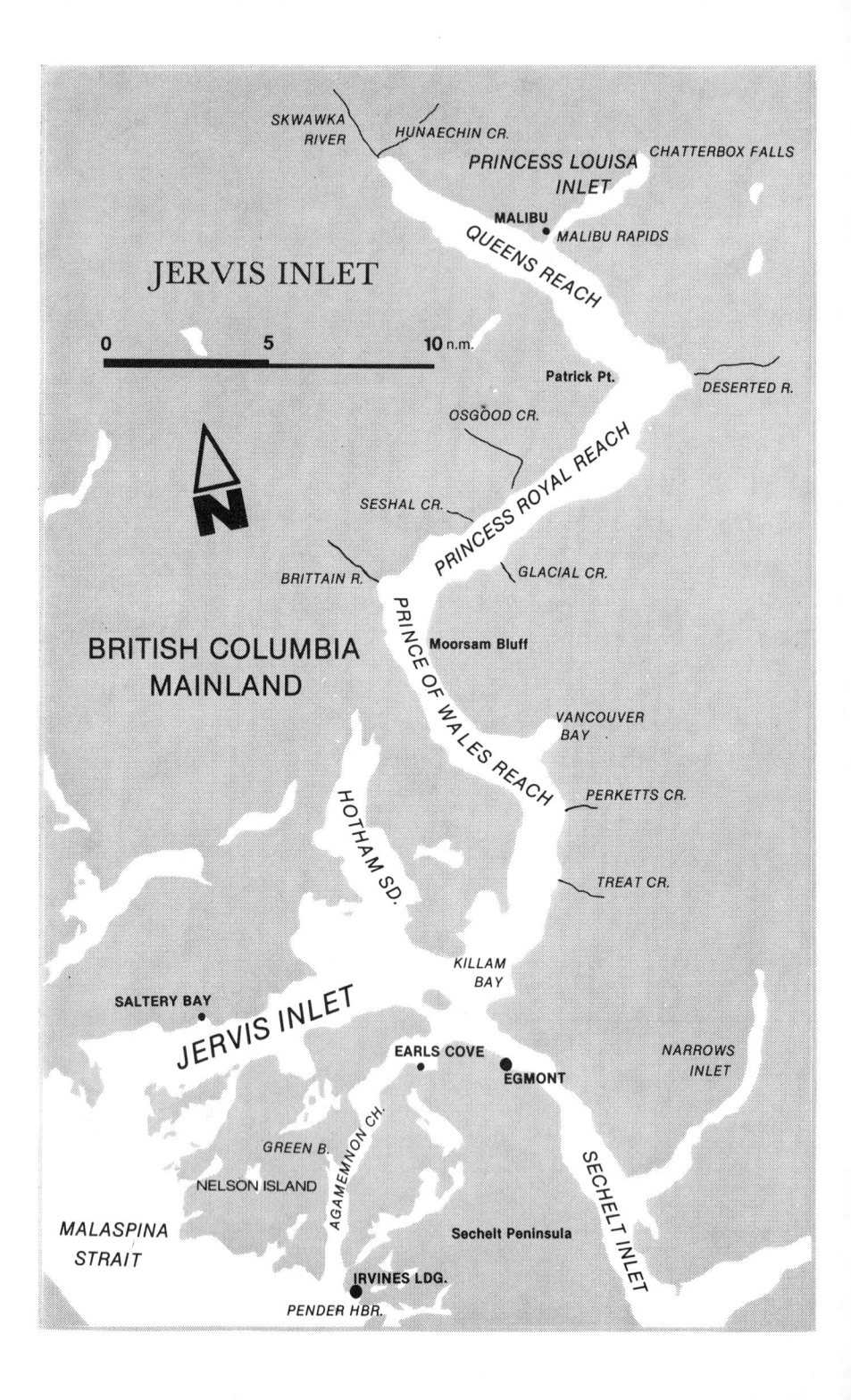

Jervis Inlet

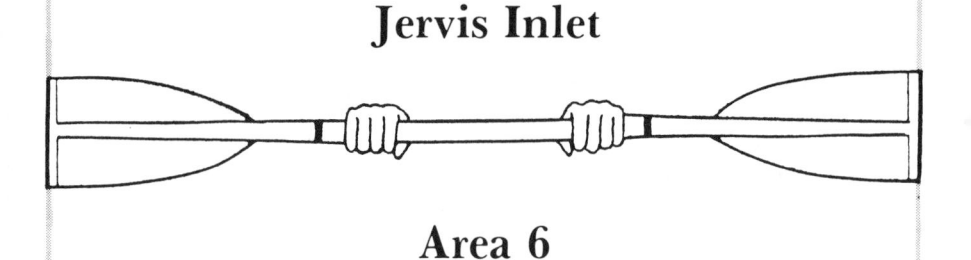

Area 6

Attractions: Inlet scenery that is internationally renowned: cliffs, waterfalls, glaciers, snow-capped peaks. Indian pictographs. Wildlife: bear, deer, goat and beaver. Navigable rivers.

Access: Launch at the northern end of the Sechelt Peninsula, either at the Earls Cove ferry terminal or at Egmont, which is just south of the mouth of Sechelt Inlet, or at Irvines Landing on the east side of the Sechelt Peninsula. If coming from Powell River, launch at Saltery Bay.

Seascape: A long zigzag inlet, 1½ miles wide. Winds are funnelled up and down its length. Long stretches of rockwall coastline make landing difficult.

Hazards: High winds can arise quickly and create chop, especially when wind and tide are opposed. If sailing, watch for sudden jibes caused by winds bouncing off inlet walls.

Season: April to October. Best in May, June and September. Princess Louisa Inlet is very crowded in July and August.

Length: 6 to 12 days.

Camping: Few beaches. Abandoned shoreline logging camps are the best bet. In Princess Louisa Inlet camp at the marine park at the head of the inlet.

Chart: 3589 Jervis Inlet and Approaches   1:76,400

Sechelt Area

Introduction

Boaters from all over the world have acclaimed the majestic beauty of Jervis Inlet and its offshoot, Princess Louisa Inlet. A sea kayak cruise along these sea canyons could be the highlight of your paddling experience.

A minimum of four days is required to explore the inlet, one way. Seven or eight days would be preferable. A one-way trip in Jervis Inlet is quite feasible. For collapsible kayak owners there are scheduled float plane services to many of the logging camps from Egmont and Vancouver, or you could charter a plane. A much cheaper alternative open to both hard and soft shell kayak owners is to hitch a ride with the boat traffic that regularly plies the inlet. In the summer the inlet is very busy with pleasure boaters travelling up to Princess Louisa Inlet. While the crowds can be bothersome, they almost guarantee a return passage. In the off-season, which is the best time to go, you can paddle north and be confident that one of the trawlers, tugs or even a pleasure craft will return you south. If you want to paddle up and down the inlet, allow eight days at the very least. Ten to twelve days is more reasonable.

The tides in the inlet can assist or impede the progress of your trip. Journey north with the flood and south with the ebb.

Agamemnon Channel to Prince of Wales Reach

Launching at Irvines Landing in Pender Harbour (famous for its salmon fishing) will add a day or two to the trip. Agamemnon Channel bustles with boat traffic, largely commercial, and the scenery does not compare with that further north. However, there are two pictographs en route. The first, just north of the round point across the channel from Green Bay, is in a rocky panel above the steeply sloping shore. The second is on a rock gallery a metre above high water level, just before the southern entrance to Earls Cove, adjacent to the fathom reading 58 on marine chart 3589.

Entering Jervis Inlet the view north is spectacular: numerous jagged peaks with mighty Mt. Churchill in center stage. There is a tumble-down shack and log dump at Killam Bay, and further north at Treat Creek, a massive scar in the hill indicates a mining operation. A half mile north of Perketts Creek look for a pictograph. In 1792 Captain Vancouver dropped anchor and spent the night at the big bay which cuts into the cliffs on the east side of Prince of

Jervis Inlet

Wales Reach, and which now bears his name. Many logging roads and trails lead into the mountains behind Vancouver Bay. If you are lucky you might spot a mountain goat on the immense bluffs which wind around the inlet north of Vancouver Bay. Directly across the inlet from Moorsam Bluff is a pictograph of an ancient canoe.

Princess Royal Reach

A deep valley penetrates the mountains at Brittain River, the site of a minimum security prison. Tail winds can die or head winds can arise as you turn the corner into Princess Royal Reach. Many of the logging camps which the chart indicates as abandoned are active again. The industrial relics surrounding these sites tell a fascinating history of logging technology.

Waterfalls spilling down the cliff faces are welcome compensation for the rain. A sunny day and the streams disappear. Southwest of Glacial Creek logging camp are the Soda Water Falls, so named because of the bubbly effect the cascading stream has on the sea.

Heading north, the scenery is all vertical. From the shoreline the mountains rise abruptly to towering peaks. On the west side of the inlet, midway between Seshal Creek and Osgood Creek, four to five metres above the high water line, is another pictograph. It is very difficult to find. Three miles further north (2¾ miles before Patrick Point), under a sheer cliff with an overhanging ledge, is another pictograph. Native men once had to dive from this ledge to prove their manhood.

Near the mouth of the Deserted River is the Native Environmental Studies Project, an inspired educational program for native and non-native secondary students from the Sechelt area. The curriculum focuses on environmental appreciation, native arts, and outdoor skills. Deserted River is navigable for a dozen paddle strokes and if you can get past the moderate rapids, for another 1.2 miles. With further portages you can reach the lakes upstream which are inhabited by much wildlife, including beaver. Alternatively, a road leads through the Indian reserve to the lakes. Ask for permission at the school to use the road.

The isolated stretches of Canada's west coast attract many colourful characters. A kayaker meets many of them. We found one here in Jervis Inlet. We were cooking dinner at a campfire on the beach when a form emerged from the shadows in the forest. Without introducing himself, a silver-haired old fellow sat by the fire and began a monologue which lasted all evening. Story after story tumbled from his lips: how he had fended off a grizzly with a shovel, how he had lost three wives, how arthritis had converted him from logging to writing "but only for the New York Times." We were enthralled. But he was not talking to us. He was talking to himself. Even after we said goodnight and crawled into the tent he chattered on.

Queens Reach

Mt. Alfred, wearing a glacier coat, looks over the final stretch of Jervis Inlet. Camping spots along Queens Reach are scarce, though some flat ground can usually be found at creek mouths. Logging scars are more visible here than elsewhere in the inlet.

Malibu, where Princess Louisa Inlet meets Queens Reach, is a fascinating place. In the 1940's a California millionaire built a luxurious resort for his Hollywood friends (hence the name), but the venture proved unprofitable and it was sold to Young Life, a religious organization, which operates it in the summer as a youth camp. As many as five hundred visitors throng the handsome log buildings in July and August. There is a wharf on either side of the rapids.

Old Man's Beard is the aptly-named plant that hangs down in long colourful whiskers from the trees at water's edge. We saw more of it on the north side of Queens Reach than anywhere else on Canada's west coast. One fine specimen completely draped its supporting tree.

A few miles from Malibu, on the north side of Queens Reach, is the largest of the Sechelt pictographs, and it is the easiest to find. If you want to see only one pictograph, this is it. Find the floating logging camp in the bay next to a steeply rising logging road. The pictograph is beyond the logging camp, where the bay starts its indentation. The rust-coloured graphics are behind the rocky ledge, approximately five metres above the water.

Skwawka River at the end of Queens Reach can be paddled as far as the junction with the Hunaechon River. It is a refreshing change from the sometimes overpowering grandeur of the inlet to follow the softer, winding course of the river. Watch for bears, attracted by the nearby logging camp and the fish in the river.

Salad bar

Princess Louisa Inlet

This is the jewel of the coastal inlets. The attraction of Princess Louisa Inlet is more than spectacular scenery. There is a special ambiance to the place. It has soul. The Malibu Rapids flush you into a vast rock bowl. You are enclosed. Smooth, polished cliffs rise 1,000 metres and spout delicate liquid strings. Only the gush of Chatterbox Falls at the end of the inlet intrudes upon the quiet serenity here.

In spite of its imposing visage of rock and water, you sense the vulnerability of Princess Louisa Inlet. That feeling inspired the creation of a conservation organization, the Princess Louisa International Society in 1953. The special charm of Princess Louisa was just too great to leave unprotected. Unbelievably, Princess Louisa is in trouble. Already logging scars fringe the mountainside atop Malibu Rapids. Further logging is planned.

Entry and exit to the inlet must coincide with slack tide at Malibu Rapids. As the chart indicates, high water slack occurs ten to fifteen minutes after high water at Point Atkinson; low water slack occurs twenty to fifty minutes after low water slack at Point Atkinson. Captain Vancouver never made it into Princess Louisa Inlet. He believed Malibu Rapids to be a river. A pictograph is located on the south shore about one mile from the rapids. It is on a sheer wall near a trickle of water.

There are a few camping spots within Princess Louisa Inlet. Most campers head for Princess Louisa Marine Park at the head of the inlet, next to Chatterbox Falls, a semi-developed park designed mainly for the scores of pleasure boaters who cruise here in the summer. There are numerous floats, a large picnic hut, toilets and fire wood. Almost any time of the year you are likely to find a yacht moored here. The water temperature of the inlet in the summer is comfortable for swimming, or try a wet slide down the flat spillway of the waterfall which is east of Chatterbox Falls.

Princess Louisa was the home of another wilderness character, James F. Macdonald, called "Mac." This vagabond/businessman/ recluse lived adjacent to Chatterbox Falls in a log cabin and then on a houseboat between 1927 and 1953. For the full story see *Mac and the Princess* by Bruce Calhoun.

Chatterbox Falls

Chapter Six
THE CENTRAL COAST

The maze of islands, channels and inlets between the northern end of Georgia Strait and the northern tip of Vancouver Island offers a remarkable range of sea kayaking opportunities. You can cruise in the shadows of British Columbia's highest peaks, mingle with a pod of orca (killer) whales, ride wild sea rivers and swim in waters that in the summer can be as warm as the Caribbean. Ashore, you can hike an overgrown logging road through a lush evergreen valley or up to a mountain lake, or practice your gourmet skills with your harvest of salmon, prawn or oyster. Though far from urban sprawl, the wilderness here has a human dimension. You will encounter the hardy folk who inhabit the region in isolated farms, lumber and fish camps and Indian settlements. And there is history here. You will find it at abandoned canneries, homesteads and Indian sites. For an account of the history of the region, see *Evergreen Islands* by Doris Andersen.

In this chapter we discuss five of the choicest sea kayaking areas on the central coast: Desolation Sound, the Discovery Islands, Knight Inlet, Western Johnstone Strait and Kingcome Inlet. There are many other fine cruising possibilities. Bute Inlet, a majestic fjord which twists through a dazzling mountain range, offers a challenging paddling cruise. If you are a bird watcher or are interested in Indian archeological sites, consider a tour to the archipelago of islands that stretches from Port Hardy to the north end of Vancouver Island. Finally, advanced sea kayakers might consider an exploration of Seymour and Belize Inlets. This vast inlet labyrinth, blocked by the barely navigable Nakwakto Rapids, is so remote that much of the sea is unsurveyed.

Many new sea paddlers undertake their first kayaking tour on the protected waters of Desolation Sound. To tour everywhere else in the central coast region safely, previous kayak touring experience is essential. Tricky tidal currents, tidal rapids, unpredictable winds, long stretches of unsheltered coastline and heavy marine traffic are some of the hazards encountered here.

DESOLATION SOUND

TOBA RIVER

0   2   4   6   8 n.m.

N

TOBA   INLET

BRITISH COLUMBIA
MAINLAND

ATTWOOD BAY

CHANNEL IS.

HOMFRAY CR.

PRYCE CHANNEL

PENDRELL SOUND

EAST REDONDA
ISLAND

REDONDA BAY

Bishop Pt.

WEST REDONDA
ISLAND

WADDINGTON CHANNEL

LLOYD CR.

LEWIS CHANNEL

TEAKERNE ARM

CASSEL L.

ROSCOE BAY

HOMFRAY CHANNEL

BLACK L.

PRIDEAUX HAVEN

TENEDOS
BAY

REFUGE
LAGOON

UNWIN LAKE

DESOLATION SOUND

REFUGE COVE

SQUIRREL COVE

PORTAGE COVE

CORTES ISLAND

GALLEY
BAY

Gifford

POWELL LAKE

Peninsula

ISABEL BAY

MALASPINA INLET

GRACE HBR.

CORTES BAY

OKEOVER IN.

COPELAND

ISLANDS

OKEOVER LDG.

LUND

Desolation Sound

Area 7

Attractions: Majestic landscapes. Oysters galore. Comfortable summertime swimming. Shoreline lakes. Largest coastal marine park. Indian pictographs.

Access: From Vancouver, two car ferries (Horseshoe Bay-Langdale and Earls Cove-Saltery Bay) and Highway 101 will take you 142 km north to Powell River. Drive 23 km further north and launch at the village of Lund. Alternatively, turn right at Malaspina Road, 6 km before Lund, and drive 4 km to the public wharf at Okeover Inlet. From Vancouver Island there are two access routes. Take the ferry from Comox to Powell River and launch at Lund or Okeover. Or take the ferry from Campbell River to Quadra Island and another ferry from Quadra to Cortes Island. On Cortes, follow the signs to either Squirrel Cove or Cortes Bay. Launch at the government wharf at either spot. In the summer there are long car line-ups for the Cortes ferry.

Seascape: Protected waters, rarely rough. Maximum crossing: 1½ miles.

Hazards: Most of the shoreline is jagged rock which is covered with razor-sharp oysters. Unpredictable winds in Toba Inlet.

Season: March to October. Water warmest but most crowded from mid-June to mid-September.

Length: 3 to 10 days.

Camping: Beaches very rare. Camping spots very difficult to find. Best to look for a spot well before dark.

Note: The isthmus at Portage Cove is privately owned and portaging is strictly prohibited.

Chart: 3594 Discovery Passage, Toba Inlet
and Connecting Channels   1:75,000

The Central Coast

Introduction

Except for the Gulf Islands, Desolation Sound is the most popular cruising area on the coast. The majestic scenery and the warm protected waters are a very attractive combination. The splendid mountain landscape is similar to that found in the coastal inlets, yet there is an openness here that softens the vista, making it even more inviting. No other area on the coast offers such fine swimming. In the summer months the water warms to 26°C. Not only humans find these temperatures agreeable. So do oysters. Millions of them. One evening in Desolation Sound and you could find yourself addicted to its luxuries: a midnight swim, a distant peak spotlighted by the moon, oyster out of the shell. And you would not be the first to fall in love with the place. Every summer hundreds of boaters voyage to the sound. We found that the yachtsmen congregate at popular anchorages, so we had no difficulty finding solitude even at the height of the season.

Malaspina Peninsula

Of the recommended Desolation Sound launching sites, Okeover Landing is the most protected. Across the inlet from the government wharf, look for an Indian pictograph. The tidal current in the inlet reaches two knots, so set off on an ebb tide if possible. Launching from Lund, proceed north through the island chain of the Copeland Islands Marine Park. The west side of Malaspina Peninsula is more developed than the east side.

Okeover and Malaspina Inlets are fertile marine gardens. Oysters, cod and jellyfish abound. Do not remove oysters from any of the commercial oyster leases, designated by shoreline signs, but otherwise: bon appetit! Don't forget to check for the red tide. A few cabins dot the shores of Malaspina Inlet and some of the owners think they own the beach. Homesteaders once populated this area and the record of their rustic lifestyle is still visible: skeletal shacks, overgrown orchards, pathways that die in the bush. Isabel Bay and Grace Harbour are especially picturesque. From Grace Harbour, a short hike inland takes you to a beaver-dammed lake.

Desolation Sound Marine Park

The scenery that greets the paddler upon entering Desolation Sound is memorable. Sky-stabbing Mt. Denman is surely the most

Portage Cove

distinctive summit on Canada's west coast. The best perspectives are from the shore of the park. The park is unusual because not all of it is public property. Although the provincial government has purchased most of the private holdings, a few remain. One of these is located at a strategic spot in the park, the isthmus of land at Portage Cove. If kayakers and canoeists could portage this short land bridge, Desolation Sound would be more easily accessible from Okeover Landing. But, understandably, the private owner of the property does not want a regular stream of boat-toting paddlers stomping through his garden. Portages are strictly forbidden.

Galley Bay, a popular anchorage, was once the site of a large commune of young people who cultivated the land behind the bay. Tenedos Bay, further east, is another busy anchorage. A short walk leads to Unwin Lake, and the energetic paddler may consider a portage. At Prideaux Haven, you are sure to find a crowd. The adjacent islets offer the best views in the sound, but finding a spot to rest boat and body is difficult.

The Central Coast

Desolation Sound received an unfavourable report in the journal of the man who named it, Captain Vancouver. He thought the place gloomy and complained that the food foraging efforts of his crew were unrewarded. Moreover, "Not a fish at the bottom could be tempted to take the hook." However, a couple we met near Prideaux Haven demonstrated to us that the waters of Desolation Sound contain enough food to supply an entire navy, let alone an explorer and his crew. The two were school teachers from Seattle. They spent their summers wandering the coast in a small cabin cruiser. Equipped with crab and prawn traps, a half dozen fishing rods and scuba gear, they virtually lived off the sea. We tasted the scrumptious products of their energy and skill. First an appetizer: sauteed sea cucumber. (Underwater this animal looks like a giant caterpillar.) Next, we had a crab salad. The main course was a bouillabaisse with some exotic ingredients: red snapper, abalone, chiton and mussel. The stalk of a bull kelp, sliced into rings, garnished the meal. Ambrosia.

Sea urchin hors d'oeuvre　　　　　　　　　　*Photo: David John Smith*

Toba Inlet

The most striking feature of Toba Inlet is its water colour, an emerald green like an alpine lake. This distinct hue is the blend of the seawater and glacial streams, which tumble out of the perpendicular mountain walls. Look for the waterfall three miles past Snout Point. Toba Inlet is off-course from Desolation Sound, both geographically and emotionally. Next to the mellow, heartwarming atmosphere of Desolation Sound, Toba Inlet is somewhat severe. The shoreline is vertical, there are few protected bays and just a solitary island. The inlet is heavily logged. The paddler and especially the kayak sailor must proceed with caution as the inlet generates its own winds.

Seventy years ago, a band of settlers tried to farm the Toba River valley, but unfavourable economic conditions and the climate killed the project. Only historic litter now attests to their efforts. Toba River is navigable for canoes and kayaks; some paddlers have ventured thirty kilometres inland. Native Indians once regularly travelled the land route between the head of Jervis and Toba Inlets by canoe and foot. Allow three days for a return excursion to Toba Inlet.

Homfray Channel to Pryce Channel

The mountainsides of Homfray Channel plummet from the sky down to the sea and continue to drop deep below the water level. Except for one other spot, the waters here are deeper than anywhere else on the coast. On East Redonda Island, directly across from Lloyd Creek, look for two pictographs, a few metres apart. At the abandoned logging camp at Homfray Creek, follow the ramshackle boardwalk through the forest to a series of waterfalls. Float planes wing in and out of the active logging camp at Attwood Bay. A hike along logging roads from Lloyd Creek and Attwood Bay will take you up to beautiful alpine meadows.

Channel Island, located at the confluence of Homfray Channel, Pryce Channel and Toba Inlet, offers excellent views of all three waterways. It is not advisable to camp there as winds can whistle out of the waterways (especially from Toba Inlet) with great velocity. The friendly panorama of Homfray Channel continues along Pryce Channel. There is a pretty waterfall close to Elizabeth Island. You can shortcut back to Desolation Sound via Waddington Channel, the passage between the Redonda Islands.

Desolation Sound, Mount Denman in distance

East Redonda Island

East Redonda Island is environmentally unique. Its Mt. Addenbroke is British Columbia's tallest offshore mountain excepting those on Vancouver Island. The astounding topography of the island packs a broad range of forest ecosystems into a small area. The right "lung" of the island is now protected as an ecological reserve, the largest land-based ecological reserve on the coast. Pendrell Sound, which penetrates the mountain island, is just as exceptional, with the warmest water on the coast, a natural oyster incubator. The coast's oyster farm industry depends on these unpolluted waters for the production of oyster spat (seed). The spat adheres to oyster shell or clay collectors suspended from numerous rafts and floats. Oyster "farmers" then collect and transport the spat to commercial oyster beds.

On a cliff just north of the tiny islands at the upper end of Pendrell Sound look for a pictograph.

West Redonda Island

There is much to explore on West Redonda Island. Look for a pictograph on Bishop Point in Waddington Channel. In Roscoe Bay, portage the short distance into Black Lake and fish for trout, or walk up the logging road behind the camp and indulge in the scenery from an elevated perspective. Groceries, liquor and fishing supplies are available at Refuge Cove. There you can portage into heavily logged Refuge Lagoon and explore its many bays. Teakerne Arm is famed for its waterfall, emptying Cassel Lake into Cascade Cove. A trail leads up to the lake.

Redonda Bay was for centuries a place of industry. An Indian fishing camp was located here and the remnants of a "stone circle" used for trapping fish are still visible at the mouth of the creek, below the high water line. White men continued the enterprise but on a larger scale, operating a fish cannery here. Inmates of a minimum security prison are the most recent occupants of the bay.

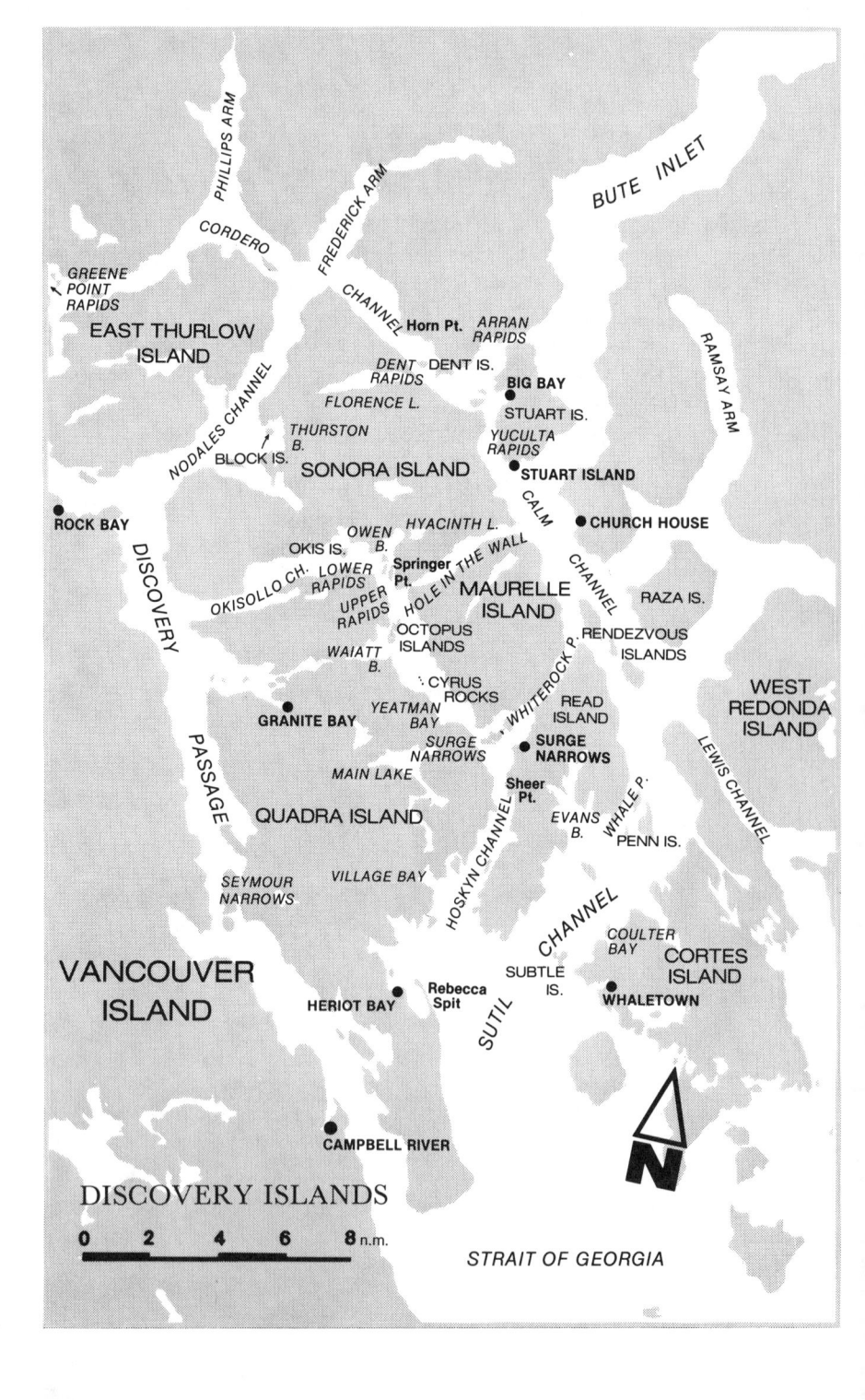

PHILLIPS ARM

CORDERO

BUTE INLET

FREDERICK ARM

RAMSAY ARM

GREENE
POINT
RAPIDS

CHANNEL

Horn Pt.

ARRAN
RAPIDS

EAST THURLOW
ISLAND

DENT DENT IS.
RAPIDS

BIG BAY

FLORENCE L.

STUART IS.

NODALES CHANNEL

THURSTON
B.

YUCULTA
RAPIDS

BLOCK IS.

SONORA ISLAND

STUART ISLAND

ROCK BAY

OWEN
B.

HYACINTH L.

CALM

CHURCH HOUSE

OKIS IS.

OKISOLLO CH.

LOWER
RAPIDS

Springer
Pt.

HOLE IN THE WALL

MAURELLE
ISLAND

RAZA IS.

CHANNEL

DISCOVERY

UPPER
RAPIDS

WAIATT
B.

OCTOPUS
ISLANDS

RENDEZVOUS
ISLANDS

CYRUS
ROCKS

WHITEROCK P.

WEST
REDONDA
ISLAND

YEATMAN
BAY

READ
ISLAND

GRANITE BAY

SURGE
NARROWS

SURGE
NARROWS

LEWIS CHANNEL

PASSAGE

MAIN LAKE

Sheer
Pt.

EVANS
B.

WHALE P.

QUADRA ISLAND

PENN IS.

SEYMOUR
NARROWS

VILLAGE BAY

HOSKYN CHANNEL

COULTER
BAY

CORTES
ISLAND

CHANNEL

SUBTLE
IS.

VANCOUVER
ISLAND

Rebecca
Spit

WHALETOWN

HERIOT BAY

SUTIL

N

CAMPBELL RIVER

DISCOVERY ISLANDS

0   2   4   6   8 n.m.

STRAIT OF GEORGIA

Discovery Islands

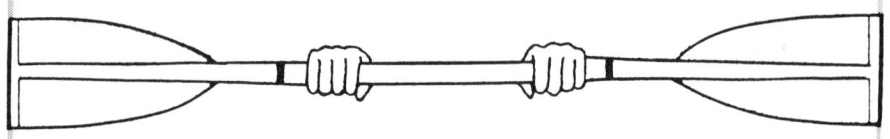

Area 8

Attractions: Sea rapids. Homesteads. Famous sports fishing. Island hiking. Sea mammals. Shoreline bluffs.

Access: Drive to the town of Campbell River 156 km north of Nanaimo on Highway 19. From Campbell River there are many launching alternatives. The best choice is Quadra Island, a short ride from Campbell River by car ferry. On Quadra follow the signs to either Heriot Bay, Village Bay or Granite Bay. If you prefer a more easterly launching spot, take the car ferry from Heriot Bay on Quadra Island to Cortes Island and then follow the signs to Whaletown or Coulter Bay. The other alternative is to launch at Rock Bay. Drive north of Campbell River on Highway 19 for 36 km. Watch for the signposted turn to Rock Bay. Turn right and follow the road for 20 km to the Rock Bay public wharf.

Seascape: Protected, narrow channels, usually calm. Tidal currents in all waterways are a major factor. No difficult crossings.

Hazards: Tidal rapids, whirlpools and overfalls, designated on the charts, are extremely dangerous to small craft except at slack tide. This trip is suitable only for adult paddlers who are experienced with the interpretation of tide and current tables and marine charts.

Season: March to October. Waters rarely crowded at any time of the year.

Length: 5 to 10 days.

Camping: Many cobblestone beaches and low, flat bluffs.

Charts: 3594 Discovery Passage, Toba Inlet
            and Connecting Channels   1:75,000
          3566 Johnstone Strait (Eastern Portion)   1:36,000
          3524 Bute Inlet   1:75,000
          Tidal current chart No. 23 for Yuculta—Dent Rapids

The Central Coast

Introduction

   Along most areas of the coast, paddlers experience an adrenalin high only in response to unexpected occurrences: a sudden storm, an unforeseen rock, the surfacing of a nearby whale. In this area, however, the adrenalin flow is not accidental. It is guaranteed. The Discovery Islands (the large group of islands located east of Discovery Passage, hence the name) squeeze the flow of tide in and out of Georgia Strait. At certain bottlenecks this flow becomes so tumultuous that it is more river than sea. But unlike their freshwater counterparts, sea rivers stop moving at the change of tide. At this time the sensible kayaker will dash through the narrows, and out into the wider channel where the current is not hazardous. Even at slack tide, the small rips, upwellings and whirlpools in the narrows make for an exciting paddle. To attempt any of the rapids at any other time than slack is to court death. In planning your dash, remember to account for the time it takes to paddle the distance of the bottleneck; some of the rapids cover two to three miles. The water may be flat as you enter the narrows, but thirty minutes later it may start to look mean. Plan to be at the *middle* of the narrows at slack. If possible, choose the slack which changes to a tide flowing in your direction, so that once the rapids have been traversed there is no danger of being pushed back in. We have travelled through the Discovery Islands at spring tides. We found that even during the springs, a cautious paddler can traverse the narrows at slack tide without significant risk.

   There is far more to the Discovery Islands than the rapids. Except near Stuart Island, where sports fishermen seek big salmon, the waterways are largely unvisited. The rapids keep away most pleasure boaters. Dolphins abound. Orca whales are common. Cod and salmon grow fat. On shore, old logging camps, mines, canneries and farms, crumbling reminders of boom and bust, invite the curious.

   Launching anywhere near Campbell River is not advisable. Turbulent Seymour Narrows would be treacherous even without the perpetual rush-hour marine traffic. Launch instead on Quadra Island or Cortes Island. Although each of these islands is populated in the south, their northern halves are wilderness. Of the two, Quadra is preferable as it involves only one ferry trip. In the summer, the small Cortes ferry is hopelessly inadequate for the car traffic. Launching at Rock Bay on Vancouver Island or Granite Bay on Quadra Island involves a long drive over logging roads.

Sutil Channel to Calm Channel

Look for a large seal colony on the islets off the Subtle Islands near Cortes Island. Evans Bay is a must for shellfish lovers. There are lots of crabs, clams and oysters in the muddy coves that indent Read Island in Evans Bay. Do not trespass on the commercial shellfish beds which are indicated by signs. From the government wharf, a four-mile logging road leads across Read Island to Surge Narrows, a fine walk through dark forests (a large block of which is destined to be logged) and past old homesteads, many of which have recently been revived. Read Island gained notoriety in the late 19th century as a result of two well-publicized murder cases, real Wild West tales complete with Winchester toting "posses," undercover agents and courtroom antics.

The Penn Islands offer exquisite views, and you might spot dolphins or whales in Whale Passage. There are a few camping spots and fallen shacks along the east coast of Read Island. Threadlike Whiterock Passage, separating Read from Maurelle Island, is navigable. The view down Whiterock Passage to the mountains of Vancouver Island is spectacular. Equally so is the view across the Rendezvous Islands to precipitous Raza Island and the mainland peaks in the distance. The tall-spired church and the pastel-coloured houses at the quaint Indian village of Church House seem frail and lonely amidst the mainland's grandeur.

Bute Inlet

The long inlet which snakes north behind Stuart Island through some of the highest mountains on the coast never fails to inspire awe. Experienced sea kayakers will enjoy the challenge of exploring this wild waterway without a guide. Our comments are confined to a warning. The inlet has few landing spots and is legendary for the violent wind it generates, called a *Bute*. Paddlers have been forced to haul their boats up rocky bluffs to avoid the tempest. Be cautious.

Yuculta Rapids — Dent Rapids

This series of tidal rapids has confounded mariners since the days of Captain Vancouver. The modern explorer can successfully navigate this area, thanks to the tidal current charts and tables. Tidal chart No. 23, one of the few charts that details tidal currents on Canada's west coast, though bulky, is helpful here. The tidal chart plots the direction and strength of the tidal currents at each hour of the tidal cycle. The tide floods south and ebbs north. At the south end of the rapids wait for slack tide either at Stuart Island settlement or at the bay on the east coast of Sonora Island just north of Hole in the Wall. At the north end of the rapids wait for slack just before Horn Point. Tidal currents dissipate only north of this point. Within ten to fifteen minutes of slack tide the waters here can be so flat that it is hard to imagine them bubbling and boiling. Even during the springs it is possible to traverse the entire length of the rapids at slack in one go, though the current will be flowing again at the exit. A better strategy, however, is to paddle the rapids in two stages, stopping at the Big Bay settlement on Stuart Island and waiting for the next slack before proceeding.

There are many superb hikes from Big Bay. Mt. Muehle, the knob behind the bay, affords spectacular views of the rapids below, and the mountains and waterways beyond. The view up steep-sided Bute Inlet is especially memorable. Approach Mt. Muehle from the south. A trail follows the coastline south to the Stuart Island marina. North of Big Bay, follow a trail inland. Its right fork leads past Eagle Lake and down to the bay on the eastern shore of Stuart Island. Via the left fork you reach the Arran Rapids, an unforgettable white water gush.

The Yuculta Rapids are an internationally known "hot spot" for salmon. Numerous fishing resorts dot the shores of Stuart, Sonora and Dent Islands. Watch for power boats and their wakes. Do not head south through the Yucultas in a stiff southeaster as even without the current, the water south of Big Bay will be rough.

Cordero Channel

The environment changes noticeably as you paddle north out of the Yucultas. The air and water are cooler. The arbutus trees vanish. The feeling of isolation grows. Along the length of the channel and its offshoots, Frederick and Phillips Arms, the mountains drop directly into the sea. If you follow Cordero Channel west to Johnstone Strait, you must navigate the Greene Point Rapids. Though less swift than the Yucultas, they still deserve respect.

Nodales Channel to Hole in the Wall

A fine length of cliffs line the Sonora Island side of Nodales Channel. If you paddle beneath the cliffs on a sunny morning, look

Sonora Island

up and see the cliff-top trees splinter the rising sun into a thousand rays. A large marine park, divided into two large chunks that are separated by a logging camp, occupies most of the east side of Thurston Bay. Several people told us of a trail leading from ruins behind Block Island to the abandoned forestry look-out of Mt. Tucker. The only trail we found (behind a holly tree) was too overgrown for hiking. Try bushwhacking. Further south, behind the logging camp, a logging road takes you up to Florence Lake.

Nodales and Okisollo Channel are separated by a section of Discovery Passage; the tidal current flows swiftly here. The current is more consistent in mid-channel but the ship traffic there makes a shoreline paddle a better alternative, even though close to shore the water is more disturbed and you have to paddle through numerous back eddies. Cobblestone beaches are common here.

The tidal current along most of Okisollo Channel is manageable at any time. Lower and Upper Rapids and Surge Narrows, however, can be navigated only at slack tide. You can avoid the Lower Rapids by paddling north of the Okis Islands, but even here the water is pockmarked and angry, except at slack. Loggers and homesteaders have populated Owen Bay for almost a century, but few of this breed now remain and there is a forsaken, lifeless feeling here. From Owen Bay a trail leads back to Hyacinth Lake and along the coast to Springer Point. The trails cross private property.

Hole in the Wall to Surge Narrows

Hole in the Wall is the gorge dividing Sonora and Maurelle Islands. At both ends of the "hole," vast rocky bluffs rise 500 metres out of the water. Except at slack tide the current races through the narrows in and out of Okisollo Channel, and it is too dangerous for small craft. At the other end, approaching Calm Channel, the current does not exceed two knots, even during springs.

The Octopus Islands Marine Park and Waiatt Bay are highlights of this area. Here you are "trapped" between rapids, Upper Rapids and Hole in the Wall to the north and Surge Narrows to the south, and this adds to the charm of this tranquil area. The largest of the Octopus Islands are not within the marine park and numerous "Private Property" signs hammer home the point. Explore the streams and ancient logging roads which wind through the forest on Quadra Island behind the park. You might never want to leave this

Waiatt Bay, view to Maurelle Island

area. Further south, look for the seal colony at Cyrus Rocks.

Yeatman Bay is a fine spot to wait for the slack at Surge Narrows. An overgrown logging road leads up the hill to Main Lake. To the north, on Maurelle Island, look for the immense, naturally carved stone elephant: Elephant Mountain. The recommended route through Surge Narrows is via Beazley Pass (see Chart 3594). Your timing must be right here. If the wind is a strong southeaster, the water south of the rapids will be very choppy.

Hoskyn Channel

The friendly community at Surge Narrows has character. It is filled with frontier archetypes: the general store (Downtown Surge) which also sells liquor, the little school house, rusty farm machinery. A logging road links Surge with the government wharf across the island at Evans Bay, a fine walk (2½ hours return) to exercise atrophying legs.

South along Hoskyn Channel, look for the cliffs behind Sheer Point on Read Island. The kayak appears so puny beneath them. Large seal colonies inhabit the islets and rocks at the south end of the channel. The marine park at Rebecca Spit has fine beaches but, back in civilization, camping is prohibited.

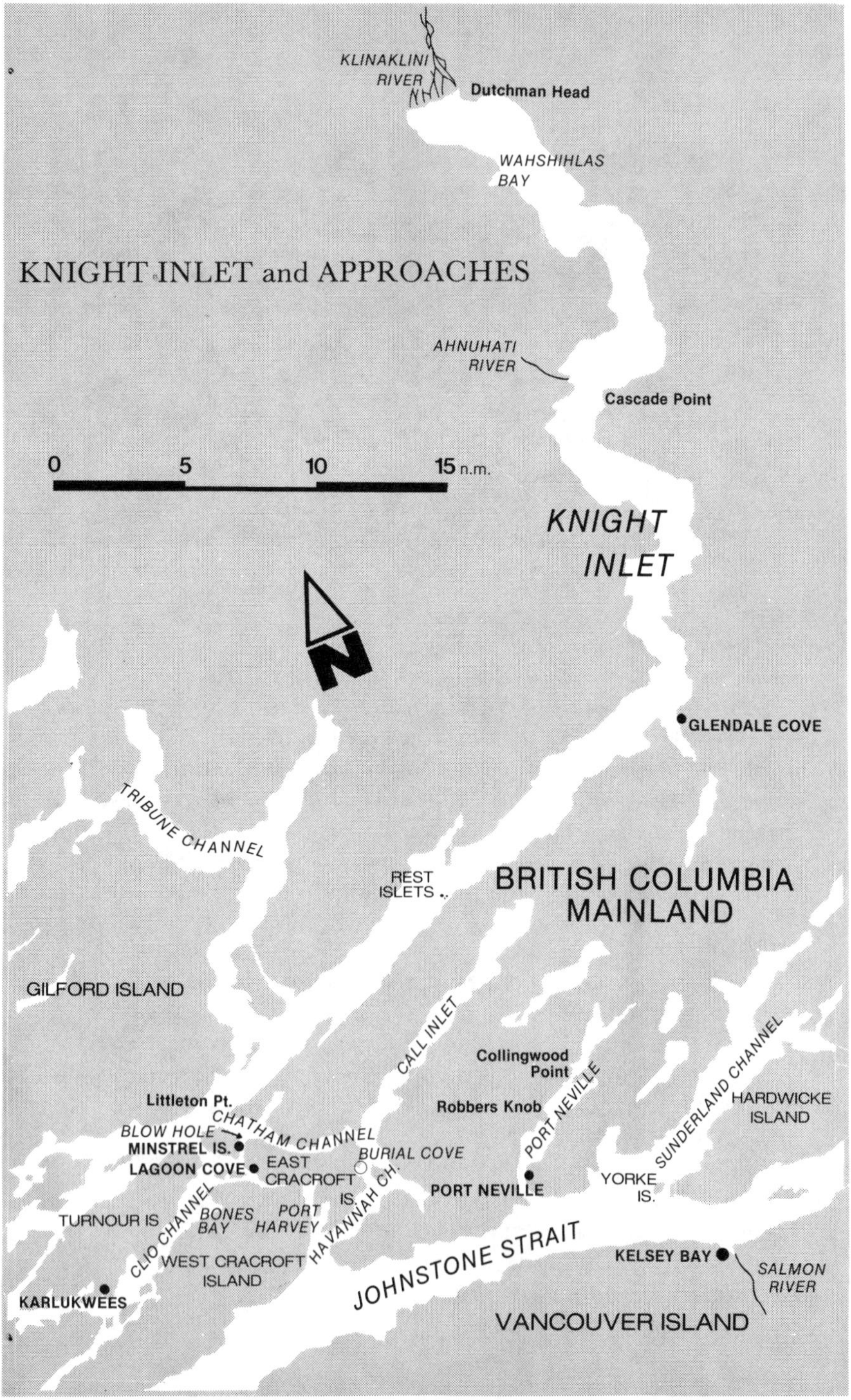

KNIGHT INLET and APPROACHES

KLINAKLINI RIVER

Dutchman Head

WAHSHIHLAS BAY

AHNUHATI RIVER

Cascade Point

0   5   10   15 n.m.

KNIGHT INLET

N

GLENDALE COVE

TRIBUNE CHANNEL

REST ISLETS

BRITISH COLUMBIA MAINLAND

GILFORD ISLAND

CALL INLET

Collingwood Point

Robbers Knob

PORT NEVILLE

SUNDERLAND CHANNEL

HARDWICKE ISLAND

Littleton Pt.

CHATHAM CHANNEL

BLOW HOLE

MINSTREL IS.

LAGOON COVE

EAST CRACROFT IS.

BURIAL COVE

HAVANNAH CH.

PORT NEVILLE

YORKE IS.

TURNOUR IS

CLIO CHANNEL

BONES BAY

PORT HARVEY

WEST CRACROFT ISLAND

JOHNSTONE STRAIT

KELSEY BAY

SALMON RIVER

KARLUKWEES

VANCOUVER ISLAND

Knight Inlet and Approaches

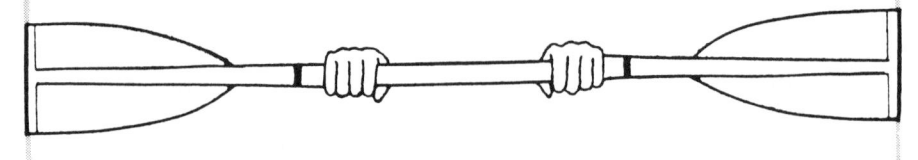

Area 9

Attractions: Scenic grandeur rivalling Lake Louise in the Rocky Mountains. Challenging seas. Native oolichan harvest in early spring. Petroglyphs and pictographs. Distinctive, isolated settlements: Glendale Cove, Minstrel Island, Port Neville.

Access: The recommended trip is a one-way paddle to or from the head of Knight Inlet, with float plane transport the other way. Rigid kayaks can be shipped in or out of the inlet. Drive to either Kelsey Bay, 235 km north of Nanaimo on Highway 19, or to Port McNeill or Beaver Cove, both approximately 350 km north of Nanaimo on Highway 19. Plane transport arrangements will dictate the exact departure point.

Seascape: Long, narrow inlet and channels. Longest crossing: 2 miles. Water unpredictable and often wild. Tidal currents always a factor.

Hazards: Winds can blow gale force with little warning in Knight Inlet. Tidal currents and ship traffic in Johnstone Strait can create big waves.

Season: March to October. The native oolichan harvest takes place in March and early April, and the snow-draped inlet is most beautiful then.

Length: 8 to 12 days, one-way (returning by plane or boat).

Camping: Beaches are rare in Knight Inlet. Try river and creek mouths or the shoreline sites of abandoned logging camps. From Minstrel Island to Kelsey Bay camping spots are more plentiful.

Charts: 3578 Knight Inlet   1:75,000
             3595 Chatham Point to Port Harvey   1:75,000
             3568 Johnstone Strait (Western Point)   1:36,000

Introduction

For adventurous sea kayakers, this trip is a must. The early spring is the best time to paddle here, as after a snowfall the north end of Knight Inlet must be one of the most majestic spots on the planet. This is also the time of the native oolichan harvest.

The inlet pokes so far inland that the climate of its upper reaches is more continental than coastal. The weather along the route is inherently unstable. One turn in the inlet can bring snow, yet blue sky and sun rays may greet the paddler around the next. Knight Inlet (like Bute Inlet) is famous for its sudden storms. We got caught in one of these and were very fortunate to survive. We were sailing our kayaks in mid-channel in a moderate breeze. With little warning the winds increased to gale force, creating vicious seas. Icy gusts blew the tops off the waves; it was like kayaking into a waterfall. Things got desperate when a rudder cable snapped on one boat and the sail on another could not be collapsed. Adrenalin and muscle power got us to shore. Treat this waterway with respect.

Knight Inlet is suitable only for a one-way trip. For most kayakers, it is too long and intense to be paddled both ways. Kayakers with folding boats can be flown in or out and thereby should have no problem arranging a one-way trip. Kayakers with rigid boats will have more difficulty. There is not enough traffic in the inlet to make hitching a ride a reliable alternative. The best plan is to ship the boat into the logging camp at the head of Knight via Coast Ferries Ltd. of Vancouver, then fly in on a scheduled or charter flight. Charter flights are economical only when the passengers have a lot of gear; if the gear has already been shipped in, a scheduled flight is cheaper. Contact Air BC in Campbell River or Port Hardy for flight information.

Should you paddle up the inlet or down? In the summer, the wind is primarily inflowing, and to take advantage of it the paddler should kayak in and fly out. In the spring and fall, the inflow and outflow are of equal frequency and thus flying in is the best choice because that gives you an opportunity to inspect the route, noting possible camping spots and places of interest. The sequence of the trip description that follows assumes you are flying in and paddling out.

Upper Knight Inlet

Pilots generally curse the flying conditions in this area but acknowledge that the view from the cockpit is stupendous. Make sure your camera is loaded and close at hand during the flight.

The plane will usually land at the wharf near Dutchman Head. If the sea is too rough it will fly two miles up the Klinaklini River and land near the logging camp. A small dam makes paddling down the river very difficult. We landed on the river and arranged a ride to the wharf with a friendly logger. At the wharf other loggers told us we were crazy to travel down Knight Inlet in "those flimsy things."

In March and April, fires and fishboats along the shore near the head of the inlet indicate oolichan (or candlefish) oil production. For further information regarding the coastal oolichan harvest, see page 144. At Knight Inlet we met a kayaker who assists the natives in their ancient industry. He uses his fibreglass kayak as a bucket, fills it with a half ton of the silvery finger-length fish and then hauls the catch to shore.

Letting the tide do the work

The most spectacular stretch of the inlet is the twenty-eight miles between Klinaklini River and Glendale Cove. For that entire length the mountains rise abruptly from the shoreline to heights often exceeding 2000 metres. And the mountains please the eye: spiky peaks, knife-edge ridges, glaciers, vast bowls, endless cliffs, a distant massif. The great falls near Cascade Point have impressed man for eons and figure prominently in native mythology. Due to the precipitous topography there has been little logging of the inlet's flanks.

The old log dumps at Wahshihlas Bay and at the Ahnuhati Anchorage can accommodate tents. At both spots the panorama across the water is a knockout. Follow the logging road a few miles up the Ahnuhati River to some fine trout fishing pools. Further south, small cobblestone beaches at the mouth of the creeks offer the best camping spots.

Glendale Cove to Minstrel Island

From its contemporary deserted appearance, it is hard to believe that Glendale Cove once thrived. Decades ago, loggers, fishermen and cannery workers crowded the dance hall every Saturday night. Only a handful of people now live here. If you are equipped with a prawn trap and fifty metres of line, dinner will be tasty in Glendale Cove. There is a prawn colony there. Drop your trap at the spot marked on Chart 3595 at fathom reading 28.

The scenery on the route south to Minstrel Island is not as impressive as that north of Glendale Cove, and the labour of loggers is evident on the slopes, but the water is spectacularly clear to great depths. The underwater colours and shapes of the marine fauna that surround the Rest Islets are especially memorable. Just inside Littleton Point, across the channel from Minstrel Island, look for a pictograph.

The settlement on Minstrel Island is worth a visit. In the early decades of this century a logging outfit hugged the shores of almost every bay and cove in the region and Minstrel Island was the hub. It had a hotel, store and post office and was regularly serviced by Union Steamships. Apparently the loggers had a prodigious capacity for beer. A resident told us that the hotel still holds the provincial record for the most number of cases sold in a week, a record dating from the 1920's. Today, the hotel at Minstrel Island services the summer boating crowd and still sells beer. The shoreline houses are connected by a boardwalk and lamps are attached to the trees along the way. An old horse wanders about. Minstrel Air offers float plane tours of Knight and Kingcome Inlets, as far inland as Mt. Waddington, British Columbia's highest mountain, and the adjacent ice fields. Unfortunately, the small charter service may be discontinued.

Cracroft Islands

If your trip began in Port McNeill or Beaver Cove, you will probably return there via the lower stretches of Knight Inlet or more likely via Clio Channel. The territory at the mouth of Knight Inlet is discussed in the following two sections of this chapter: Western Johnstone Strait and Kingcome Inlet.

An early survey crew is responsible for the peculiar name places at the opening of Clio Channel: Sambo Point, Negro Rock and Bones Bay. The latter is the site of a derelict cannery, perched precariously atop a forest of rotting piles. Now used as a fishing net loft, the building is strictly off-limits to visitors, due to its hazardous state of disrepair. Behind, the "China House" once sheltered overworked coolie labourers. Empty opium bottles have been recovered from the rafters.

If you are returning to Kelsey Bay, the best route is along Chatham Channel. The current here can reach six knots; it is important to travel with the tide. The flood tide flows southeast, the ebb tide in the reverse. Note that in the current tables Chatham Channel is a secondary station on Seymour Narrows. There are overfalls near the islands in the channel, but they are easily avoided if you keep to the south side of the waterway. Look for a seal colony on the rocks off these islands. At high tide it is possible to traverse the tiny inlet that separates the Cracroft Islands, although you most portage over some dry spots. The small marine at Lagoon Cove, on the southwest end of the "Blow Hole" sells a surprising variety of frozen bread, but little else.

Loggers and native Indians once populated Port Harvey, but now it is usually deserted. Berry bushes and fruit trees can be found near the shoreline and the foreshore has buried treasure: clams. The meadows at the end of the inlet abound with waterfowl and mosquitoes. On the southwest corner of the large Mist Islet is a distinctive rust-coloured pictograph. Spirits reside at Burial Cove, on

Near Chatham Channel, shell beach

the east coast of Cracroft Island. Long ago, the Matilpi tribe disposed of their dead in the threes there.

The skies in this area seem to be permanently spotted with eagles. We camped beneath a bathtub-sized eagle's nest, its occupant a distant spy. The bird's lofty home is located on the south shore of Havannah Channel and is visible from the water.

Port Harvey and Kelsey Bay

When leaving Port Harvey, just before entering Johnstone Strait, look for a pictograph on West Cracroft Island opposite Hull Rock. With so many beaches, there should be no trouble locating camping spots along either side of Johnstone Strait. Before crossing Johnstone Strait, visit Port Neville. It is a unique pastoral sanctuary. The Hansen clan has lived here since 1891, and the little settlement exudes a pioneer charm. The buildings are constructed of logs, the grass grows waist-high in the lowland field, cows and chickens wander about. Though the surrounding area is heavily logged, in Port Neville you would never know it.

A few miles up Port Neville Inlet, just north of Robbers Nob (near where "Dols" are indicated on Chart 3595) look for a series of petroglyphs on the sandstone rocks below the high water line. Further on, just past Collingwood Point, is another set of native rock carvings.

Five miles south of Port Neville, on strategically situated Yorke Island off the western tip of Hardwicke Island, are the remains of one of the largest World War II gun emplacements and searchlights on the coast.

Caution is required in paddling down Johnstone Strait to Kelsey Bay. Even without wind, the tide can chew up the waters and digest a kayaker. In our paddle from Port Neville to Kelsey Bay the wind and tide stamped the surface of the water with a bizarre sequence of imprints: white-capped waves, whirlpools, standing waves dissolving into light chop, and the strangest of all, oceanlike swell. The tide rips propelled driftwood torpedos. We were relieved to reach the Kelsey Bay breakwater and the quiet flow of the Salmon River.

QUEEN CHARLOTTE STRAIT

GILFORD ISLAND

KNIGHT INLET

VILLAGE IS.

TURNOUR ISLAND

KARLUKWEES

MAMALILACULLA

NEW VANCOUVER

HARBLEDOWN ISLAND

WEST CRACROFT ISLAND

JOHNSTONE STRAIT

GROWLER COVE

ROBSON BIGHT

TSITIKA RIVER

BLACKFISH SOUND

BLACKNEY PASSAGE

HANSON ISLAND

TELEGRAPH COVE

BEAVER COVE

MALCOLM ISLAND

CORMORANT IS.

ALERT BAY

STRAIT

SOINTULA

BROUGHTON

PORT McNEILL

WESTERN JOHNSTONE STRAIT

VANCOUVER ISLAND

0   2   4   6 n.m.

Western Johnstone Strait

Area 10

Attractions: Robson Bight and Blackfish Sound: the largest concentration of orca whales on the coast. Tsitika River: fabulous virgin watershed and estuary. Mamalilaculla: totems and taboo.

Access: Drive to the northeast corner of Vancouver Island, approximately 350 km north of Nanaimo on Highway 19. Launch at Telegraph Cove, the spot closest to Robson Bight, or launch 25 km further north at Port McNeill. Daily flights on Pacific Western Airlines connect Vancouver and Port Hardy. Buses travel from the Port Hardy airport to Port McNeill.

Seascape: Johnstone Strait averages two miles across, has significant tidal currents and is frequently choppy.

Hazards: Much marine traffic in Johnstone Strait and Blackney Passage. Watch for boat wakes.

Season: April to October. Best in summer months.

Camping: Along the Vancouver Island side of Johnstone Strait there are many beaches. To prevent overuse of the area, avoid camping near the Tsitika River estuary. Camping spots are scarce in the islands bordering the north side of Johnstone Strait.

Note: To visit Mamalilaculla, get permission from the Mamalilaculla Indian band in Campbell River.

Charts: 3659 Broughton Strait   1:37,600
        3568 Johnstone Strait (Western Portion)   1:36,500

The Central Coast

Introduction

The orca whale, also called the killer whale or blackfish, is a magnificent creature. Its erect black dorsal fin knifes through the water like the tower of a sub. A curling wake and a series of blowhole plumes mark its course. This powerful animal has a playful, gentle side. It loves to jump and splash or scratch its back against shoreside rocks. The kayaker is well-positioned to view the whales. Although at first it is slightly unnerving to paddle near these large animals, familiarity breeds trust and the camera-clicking kayaker soon wants to get as close as possible. On occasion we have been within a paddle-length of juvenile orcas. We have heard of no boater on the coast being harmed by orca whales. For further information about the whales, see *The Whale Called Killer* by Erich Hoyt.

You can almost always find a pool of orca whales in Robson Bight or Blackfish Sound. Recently this area and its whales have received publicity in the media. The attention has been a good thing. A forestry company wanted to turn Robson Bight into a booming ground and log much of the virgin Tsitika estuary behind the bight. In response to public pressure, the provincial government has placed a moratorium on development of this area. A small, dedicated group of divers and others in the Port McNeill and Telegraph Cove area struggled for many years to protect the priceless environment of Robson Bight and the Tsitika River watershed. Their success, though still not complete, is an inspiration to wilderness conservation groups along the west coast.

Port McNeill to Telegraph Cove

If you launch at Port McNeill you will paddle east along the busy Broughton Strait. Alert Bay on Cormorant Island (six miles southeast of Port McNeill) is well worth a visit. The crossing can be difficult if the three-knot tidal current opposes the frequent winds here. For over a century the native and white cultures have crossed paths at Alert Bay. The co-existence has frequently been unhappy, especially when the white man has tried to prohibit the potlach ceremony which the Kwakiutls valued so highly. Today, Alert Bay is an interesting mosaic of brown faces, white faces, fishboats, heritage buildings (see especially the longhouse) and totem poles. The two cultures no longer seem incompatible. The native ceremonies are now good for business, attracting a throng of cruise ship visitors.

Telegraph Cove is a sleepy place that somehow seems out of tune with the 1980's. Most of the buildings in the shoreline village are on stilts; the tide rises and falls underneath. A boardwalk twists around these structures, past colourful flower boxes, and leads to the post office and wharf. There a group of divers showed us their catch from the floor of the cove: old dinner dishes stamped with the imprint of the Union Steamship Company. Across the cove, an antique mill — a mass of gears, fly wheels and saw blades — ingests long barky tree trunks and spits out smooth lumber.

Robson Bight

You can paddle to Robson Bight from Telegraph Cove in a day. It is very difficult to time your departure with a favourable tide. The currents here seem to defy prediction, even with the help of tide and current tables. Watch for deep-sea freighters, cruise ships, tugs and fishboats which rumble through Johnstone Strait. Towboats pulling log booms and barges regularly ply Johnstone Strait. Stay clear of such craft. They are not easily manoeuvred. Do not attempt to cross between the towboat and its load, as you may come to grief on the towing cable.

Robson Bight

Orcas are often heard before they are seen. On a calm day, their noisy breathing can be heard over a great distance. South of Robson Bight are two orca rubbing beaches where the creatures are best observed. The first one is one mile east of the eastern-most point of Robson Bight, where the shoreline makes a little indentation. The second is a mile further east of the first. Follow the coastline. If the whales are at the rocks, you cannot miss them.

One reason why the whales congregate at Robson Bight is the abundance of food. The Tsitika River is prime salmon breeding habitat. On a July trip to the bight so many of the fish were jumping that we considered giving up trolling to try to snatch them out of the air. From the intertidal zone back into the watershed, nature is exceptionally rich along the Tsitika River. On a sunny day the colour can be overwhelming. The seaweed-matted foreshore glows yellow; countless sandy rivulets add streaks of silver. The forest is a blend of greens, from the soft tint of the riverside grasses to the dark hues of the cedar and spruce. Glinting in the background are the snow-freckled peaks of Vancouver Island.

The estuary and watershed of the Tsitika River deserve at least a day. Pack a lunch and follow the river through the virgin woodland. The moss underfoot is like sponge. Wade through the rapids. Observe the waterfowl in the river ponds. Watch them depart with a flap. Dive in for a refreshing swim. Sun-bathe on the sand bars — secluded beaches in the middle of the forest. Look for the Tsitika bog, one of the largest on Vancouver Island.

The enchanted wilderness on Robson Bight and the Tsitika watershed is easily accessible and thus vulnerable. Overuse could destroy its special charm. Avoid camping near the estuary. Be especially careful with campfires. Leave no trace of your visit.

Johnstone Strait to Blackney Passage

Cross Johnstone Strait in the morning or evening when the winds are light. When strong winds arise, the sea here quickly gets rough. Tidal currents flow swiftly through Blackney Passage, between Hanson Island and West Cracroft Island. Tide rips and standing waves are common. We had an eventful paddle along Blackney Passage. As we approached Hanson Island we heard a bizarre series of screeches reverberating over the water. We were puzzled. Guided by our ears, we discovered the source of the clamor: a group of buildings on Hanson Island. It was a whale research station. The sounds we had heard were the high-pitched calls of the whales. Researchers had connected underwater microphones to the station's stereo system and then turned the volume high. Even the untrained ear could hear a dialogue in the shrill cries.

The researchers followed the whales in speedboats for hours every day. They were the first scientists to observe a non-captive orca give birth, in a cove not far from Hanson Island. They discovered that the delivery was a group effort. Immediately after the birth a number of whales nosed the newborn whale to the surface and kept it there, enabling it to breathe.

Mamalilaculla

The trip to the abandoned Indian village at Mamalilaculla takes the paddler through protected waters and a cluster of islands, valued not only for their soft beauty, but also for their archeological wealth. At one of these islands we encountered a canoeist and his dog. The fellow told us that the night before the dog had wandered out of the forest with a moss-covered human skull gripped between its jaws.

The pier and houses on Harbledown Island constitute the intermittently occupied Indian village of New Vancouver. Mamalilaculla on Village Island is a special place. In 1921 it was the site of one of the largest potlatches ever held. A potlatch is a ceremony peculiar to the native peoples of the Pacific coast from Washington to Alaska, in which the host gives away or destroys valuable articles as a testament to his wealth. The potlatch at Mamalilaculla lasted for six days. During that period Chief Dan Cranmer of Alert Bay entertained 300 guests and divided his vast wealth among them. Gifts included canoes, pool tables, musical instruments, sewing machines, motorboats and thousands of Hudson's Bay Company blankets. The RCMP stopped the event and Dan Cranmer was prosecuted under the infamous potlatch laws. It was the last major potlatch to be held on the coast.

An ominous feeling pervades Mamalilaculla today. It is dilapidated, yet dignified. Some of the houses must once have been stately. The fine lines of the old, beached gas-boat are still pleasing. The totems standing and fallen, the fluted house posts and massive beams proclaim that, while the people have left, their spirit remains.

Berries are plentiful at Mamalilaculla. We found raspberries,

Mamalilaculla

huckleberries, blueberries and salmonberries and a few cherry trees. The pathways smell of mint. People who do not have permission to visit Mamalilaculla from the band office in Campbell River risk an unfriendly reception if any band members are at the site.

There is little of interest at the abandoned village on Turnour Island, Karlukwees. The totems that once stood here have been removed.

Gas boat at Mamalilaculla

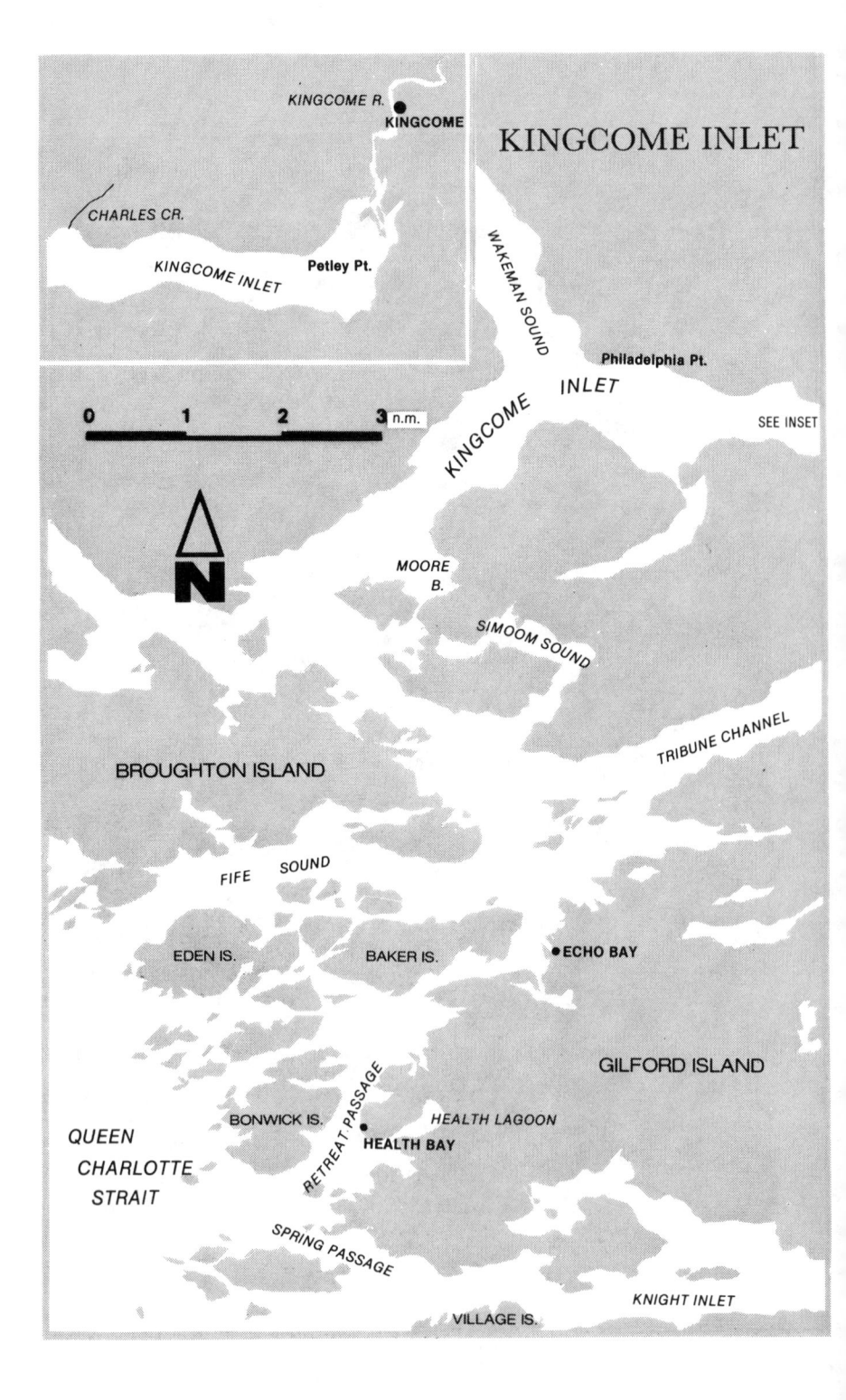

Kingcome Inlet

Area 11

Attractions: Isolated native village. Indian carvings. Cultivated river estuary. March to April: oolichan (candlefish) harvest. Excellent prawn fishing. Outpost personalities.

Access: Drive to the northeast coast of Vancouver Island, approximately 350 km north of Nanaimo on Highway 19. Launch at the town of Port McNeill or at Telegraph Cove. Daily Pacific Western Airline flights connect Vancouver and Port Hardy. Buses travel from the Port Hardy airport to Port McNeill.

Seascape: Protected waters except along the islands and passages bordering Queen Charlotte Sound. Few landing spots in steep-sided Kingcome Inlet. Sudden winds common in Kingcome Inlet and at the mouth of Knight Inlet.

Hazards: The mouth of the Kingcome River can be dangerously choppy especially during an inflowing wind.

Season: March to September. Oolichan fishery in March and early April.

Length: 7 to 14 days.

Camping: Beaches scarce. Check river and stream mouths for flat ground. Watch for wolves, grizzly and black bears in the Kingcome valley.

Charts:		
3568 Johnstone Strait (Western Portion)		1:36,500
3576 Fife Sound and Kingcome Inlet		1:37,500

The Central Coast

Introduction

The trip from Johnstone Strait to Kingcome Inlet or reverse is one of the most varied on the coast. The paddler will cross the orca whale domain of western Johnstone Strait, meander through a myriad of islands, pass Indian villages, logging camps and remote outposts, and then travel down a landslide-prone inlet to the legendary village of Kingcome.

The people can be just as interesting as the geography. Along the paddling route you will encounter a mix of personalities, from loggers to houseboaters to hermits.

The distance between Port McNeill to Telegraph Cove and the village of Kingcome can be paddled in four to five days, but the kayaker will probably want to see Robson Bight and Mamalilaculla and spend a couple of days near the Kingcome delta, so a minimum length of a one-way trip is seven to ten days. For a return journey allow two weeks.

There are many alternatives in arranging a one-way trip. If you own a collapsible kayak you can fly to the logging camp float on the Kingcome River via float plane from Port Hardy (connecting with the jet from Vancouver). Both charter and scheduled flights are available. Contact Air BC in Port Hardy. Rigid kayaks can be shipped to Kingcome from Vancouver via Coast Ferries Ltd. As no passengers are carried on this service you must fly in. This is a relatively expensive proposition, but enables you to paddle this remote area even if you can spare only a week. Alternatively, consider hitching a ride out of the inlet aboard a pleasure craft or fishboat. In the summer there is enough traffic to make this feasible, though you may have to wait a day for a ride.

Western Johnstone Strait

For details regarding this area, see page 113.

Mamalilaculla to Echo Bay

Leaving the abandoned Indian settlement of Mamalilaculla on Village Island and heading north, you will cross the mouth of Knight Inlet. Tidal currents reach three knots and the winds can blast from east or west, creating high seas. The tiny islands which puncture the waters of Spring and Retreat Passages are enchanting. The foreshore of many of the bays and lagoons here are filled with shellfish, but

Hitching a ride

check for red tide. During our trip a native died as the result of consuming contaminated butter clams from (ironically) Health Lagoon. At nearby Health Bay Indian reserve there is a modern Indian village with colourfully painted houses. The village's treasure is a large ceremonial dugout canoe.

Camping sites in this area are difficult to find. We searched for a couple of hours one night and the only flat spot we could find was atop a duck hunter's float in a secluded cove. The next morning, as we were preparing to leave our floating camp, a Canada Fisheries patrol vessel motored into the cove and the Fisheries Officers and his wife treated us to fresh coffee, steaming muffins and entertaining fishing tales.

At Echo Bay you will find a store, lodge, post office and bar. Unfortunately, the bar is not open on a regular basis. A large field, covering a huge Indian midden, occupies much of the Echo Bay Marine Park. Archeological studies indicate that man has lived here for thousands of years.

Houseboats, some of elaborate construction with cantilever roofs and plexiglass dome windows, are nestled along the shores of Echo

Bay and Simoom Sound, a few miles north. While waiting for the store to open at Echo Bay we met a kayaker of some reknown, "Kayak Bill." He had left Vancouver seven years previously, intending to paddle to the Queen Charlottes. He got waylaid at appropriately-named Eden Island, one of the islands nearby. A confirmed hermit, he was proud of his self-sufficiency. He told us that the land and sea give him everything he needs except "tobacco, flour and milk powder."

Outer Islands

The countless uninhabited islands that cluster at the east end of Queen Charlotte Strait are off-course for most boaters and thus are perfect for the kayaker who wants to enjoy the marine environment in solitude. Many of the rocks and islets here are rookeries for seal and sea lions. Try fishing along the reefs.

Kingcome Inlet

Broughton Island, at the mouth of the inlet, is fringed with lagoons — saltwater lakes that open to the sea, usually through narrow, fast-flowing channels. They are haunted places. As the forest starts abruptly at the water's edge, they are beachless.

Luxurious pleasure craft frequently visit the British Columbia Forest Service float in Moore Bay. When we berthed at the float, a dinner-jacketed yachtsman interrupted his deckside cocktail and gave us the salmon he had just hooked off the stern of his cruiser. We considered smoking the fish in the smokehouse located in the woods behind the float, but our appetites vetoed such an experiment. The prawn fishing in Moore Bay is excellent. Some friends set a prawn trap in the middle of the bay. The next morning it was stuffed with three dozen prawns. Imagine, a kilo of fresh prawn, free for the taking!

As you venture up Kingcome Inlet, a massive landslide near Philadelphia Point will catch your eye. The steep slopes of the inlet are cut with many such natural scars. Camping spots along the inlet are extremely rare. Charles Creek is the best refuge if the sea gets mean. The pipes, piles and boilers indicate the site of a once-important cannery here. A rough survey trail parallels the creek back into the mountains. Perched on the rocky point west of the creek is a brightly-coloured Indian memorial: the sea claimed a number of lives near this spot.

Kingcome Delta

The Kingcome River mouth is a place of contrasts. The broad, flat delta challenges the otherwise vertical terrain. The trees that grow on the delta are stunted, like bonsai, yet on the nearby mountains massive evergreens push skyward. And in the lap of this rugged wilderness you find a reassuring farmhouse, a pasture and sad-eyed cows. This is the Halliday farm, operated today by the descendants of the homesteaders who arrived in 1895.

The waters at the head of the inlet, fed by glacial streams, are thick and icy — like a daiquiri. Choppy waters are common where the river meets the sea. Returning from a moonlight paddle, we got caught in standing waves here. After this experience we were prepared to believe the stories we had heard about the sea swallowing fishing boats at the river mouth. The public float near Petley Point is one of the few camping possibilities in the area. Ask local mariners to point out the location of the nearby Indian pictographs.

The main channel of the river begins on the west side of the inlet and winds through the estuary to the floats near the logging camp. In the summer, if the horseflies were not so hungry here, one would be tempted to explore the network of marshland canals.

Kingcome Village

Three miles north of the government float is the Kingcome village, immortalized in the novel *I Heard the Owl Call My Name* by Margaret Craven. Largely as a result of this fine novel, pleasure boaters now regularly visit Kingcome village. These people will moor their yachts in the inlet and zoom upstream in noisy runabouts. It is no wonder that the local people are now suspicious of visitors. We arrived at the village late in the afternoon, pulling our kayak ashore beside a villager's dugout canoe. We immediately paid our respect to the young chief. He made it clear that, though we could look around, we were not welcome. Later, a friendly village elder invited us into his home, and so our evening with his family was the highlight of the trip.

Our host gave us a guided tour through a century of native Indian history. His great-grandparents had fought tribal battles. In one such conflict, an Indian village near Health Bay was raided by a north

Kingcome Village

coast tribe. A crazy old woman at the Kingcome village saw the battle in her dreams and convinced a group of young men to paddle to Health Bay to investigate. On their way they encountered the plunderers and still more blood was spilled. Our host could remember when the dugout canoe was the only means of transport, and when only his native language was spoken in the village. It was in his lifetime that the native people were given the vote. Unlike some of his fellow villagers, our host harboured no resentment of white people, perhaps because he had succeeded in their world. He was active in politics and had done well in business, preferring the capitalist's ethic to the collectivist ways of his people. Just before we left, he showed us a Kwakiutl treasure — a piece of the crest-engraved "copper." In former times Indians would trade the equivalent of thousands of blankets for a copper.

If the Indian band grants permission to visit Kingcome do not loiter or camp in the village. See the totem poles and the carvings in the church and then move on. Cameras can be offensive. You can continue upriver or travel back to the delta. Bears are a frequent concern in the Kingcome valley. During our visit, villagers sighted two silver-tipped grizzlies. Remove your food bags from the boat and stash them away from the camp.

In March and early April, the river mouth is bustling with the native oolichan harvest. For details regarding the phenomenal coastal oolichan run, see page 144 .

Chapter Seven
THE NORTH COAST

Most of Canada's west coast lies north of Vancouver Island. This vast maritime wilderness is a long distance from civilization, and that is its main charm. You may occasionally share the sea with a passing trawler, tug or cruise ship, but mostly you will ply these remote waters in solitude. Days, even weeks of paddling can separate the tiny villages which dot the coast. Between the friendly outposts, your only company will be nature.

A four hundred kilometre long barrier of offshore islands shelters all but a few stretches of the north coast. The very scenic inside passage which parallels this coast is an increasingly popular long-distance (one to two months) paddling route. For those kayakers with more restricted time schedules there are also many trip options in this region. This chapter discusses the two areas which we feel are of the most interest in the north coast, and which are easily accessible, thanks to regular passenger ferry and float plane services. The first is the vast galaxy of islands surrounding the villages of Bella Bella and Ocean Falls, and the second is the anthropologically fascinating Nass Bay at the northern tip of Canada's west coast.

There are, of course, many other fine cruising areas and we will briefly discuss them here. A challenging stretch of open ocean extends fifty kilometres along the mainland coast from the northern tip of Vancouver Island to Calvert Island — the only significant length of mainland coastline where offshore islands provide no protection. From Captain Vancouver who, in 1792, almost lost his ship *Discovery* just south of the prominent point he named Cape Caution, to the modern ferry skippers whose passengers are often seasick due to the rolling seas, mariners have always been wary of these unsheltered waters. Kayakers who venture along this coast will find many rewards beyond the challenging seas, including abandoned Indian villages, totem poles, and long sandy beaches.

The north coast is stabbed by many long inlets, all of which are rarely visited by kayakers, due to their inaccessibility. The waterways that probe inland near Rivers Inlet are famed for their salmon fishing. Sports fishermen from all over the world travel to the lodges seeking the big spring salmon which populate the waters. Rivers Inlet is accessible only by plane. Further north, the spectacularly beautiful series of inlets near the mainland village of Bella Coola can be reached by car, but only after an almost four hundred kilometre drive over dirt roads through central British Columbia. An added feature of an excursion in the Bella Coola waterways are shoreline hot springs at three different locations; see *Hotsprings of Western Canada* by Jim McDonald. Hot springs are the main attraction in the inlets leading to the mill town of Kitimat. In two weeks of paddling you can visit seven different thermal springs in this area; consult the above-mentioned book. Kitimat is accessible by paved highway.

The two long, slender waterways that make up almost half the length of the north coast inside passage, Princess Royal Channel and Grenville Channel, are highlights on the inside passage route. These scenic wilderness canals inspire poetic description by everyone who voyages along them. For those not paddling the entire length of the inside passage route, these waterways are very difficult to get to, accessible only by float plane from Prince Rupert.

Finally, there is much of interest on the doorstep of Prince Rupert. Just five kilometres east of the town, along Venn Passage, you will find a concentration of Indian petroglyphs. For details see *Indian Petroglyphs of the Pacific Northwest* by Beth and Ray Hill. The string of islands leading to the village of Kitkatla, 72 kilometres south of Prince Rupert, displays many intriguing relics of the succeeding generations of pioneers who once settled there.

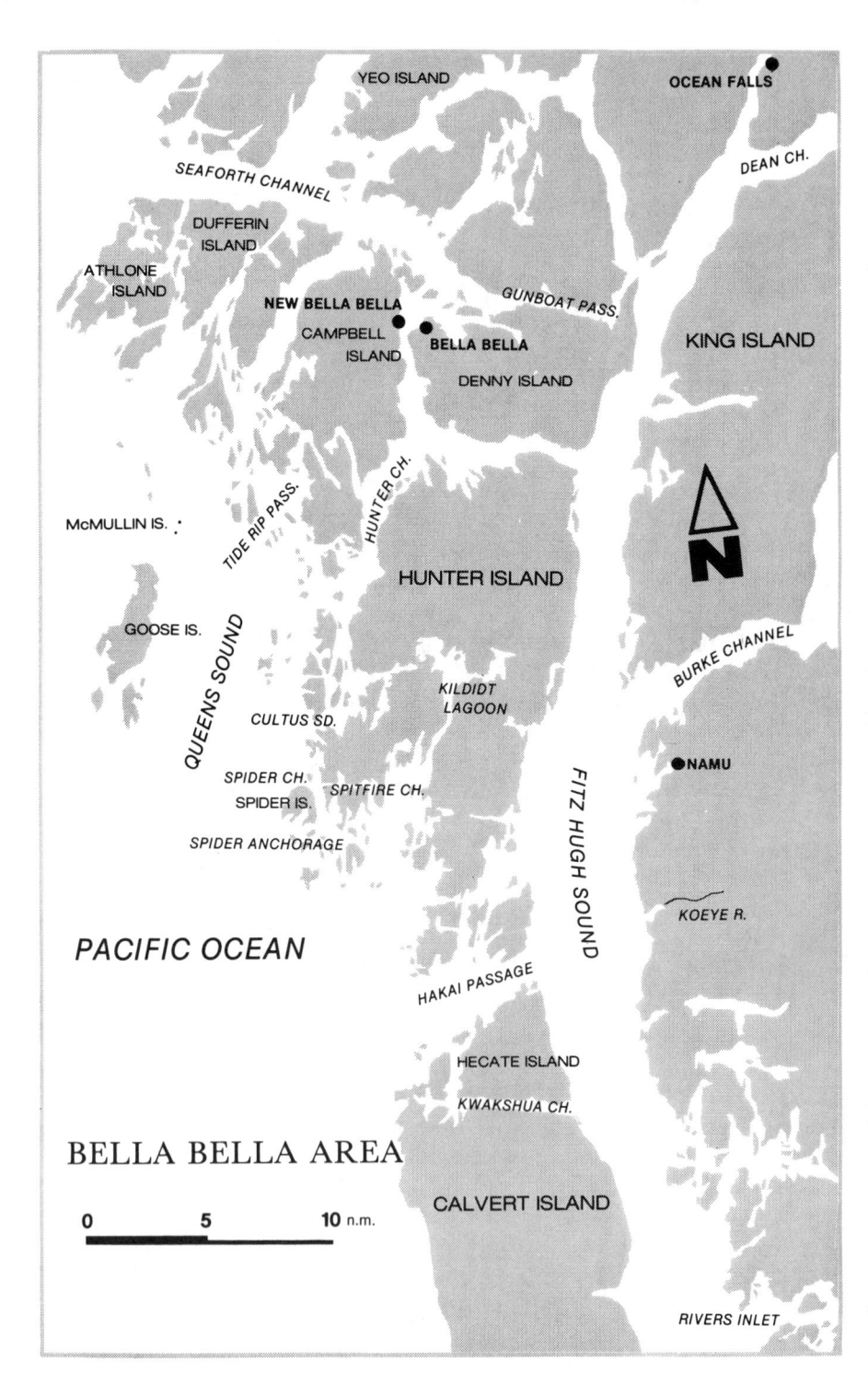

YEO ISLAND

OCEAN FALLS

SEAFORTH CHANNEL

DEAN CH.

DUFFERIN
ISLAND

ATHLONE
ISLAND

GUNBOAT PASS.

NEW BELLA BELLA

KING ISLAND

CAMPBELL
ISLAND

BELLA BELLA

DENNY ISLAND

HUNTER CH.

McMULLIN IS.

TIDE RIP PASS.

N

HUNTER ISLAND

GOOSE IS.

BURKE CHANNEL

QUEENS SOUND

KILDIDT
LAGOON

CULTUS SD.

NAMU

SPIDER CH.   SPITFIRE CH.

SPIDER IS.

FITZ HUGH SOUND

SPIDER ANCHORAGE

KOEYE R.

PACIFIC OCEAN

HAKAI PASSAGE

HECATE ISLAND

KWAKSHUA CH.

BELLA BELLA AREA

0   5   10 n.m.

CALVERT ISLAND

RIVERS INLET

Bella Bella Area

Area 12

Attractions: Placid lagoons, back to back with the open Pacific Ocean. Golden beaches on desolate islands. Exceptionally rich bird life. Friendly, boardwalked fishing village. Indian carvings. First rate salmon fishing. Challenging open water crossings.

Access: The British Columbia Ferry Corporation connects Bella Bella and Ocean Falls with Port Hardy in the south or Prince Rupert in the north. Air BC services Ocean Falls, Shearwater (near Bella Bella) and Namu from Port Hardy or Vancouver. Trans-Provincial Airlines flies to Bella Bella from Prince Rupert.

Seascape: The most diverse seascape on the coast. Open ocean and inside waterways. Lagoons everywhere. Queens Sound and Fitz Hugh Sound: each a 5 mile crossing.

Hazards: Swell along the exposed coastline. Surf on the exposed beaches. Tide rips where the inside channels and passages meet the ocean.

Season: May to September. June is the driest month.

Length: 7 to 21 days.

Camping: Beach camping on Goose and Calvert Islands. Camping sites are scarce everywhere else. Fresh water very scarce on lowland islands. Both grizzly and black bears may be encountered on the mainland.

Charts:		
3720 Idol Point to Ocean Falls		1:41,100
3727 Cape Calvert to Goose Island		1:73,600
Including Fitz Hugh Sound		1:73,600
3728 Milbanke Sound and Approaches		1:76,600
3785 Namu Harbour to Dryad Point		1:40,500
3786 Queens Sound and Approaches		1:36,500
3787 Queens Sound to Seaforth Channel		1:36,400

The North Coast

Introduction

It is an exhilerating sensation to land your kayak on a shore that has never known the footsteps of man. You experience that sensation repeatedly on a tour of the vast archipelago of islands surrounding the remote village of Bella Bella. These offshore islands have the character of an exile. They seem to have been banished not only from the mainland, but from time as well. Except near Bella Bella the lonely territory shows no sign of man — no logging, no roads, not even a shack. For countless eons this territory has been exactly as you will find it today: isolated, lonely, wild. It is difficult to paddle among these islands and not sense something primordial, something eternal. After a couple of weeks here you will feel closer to the stars than to urban civilization three hundred kilometres away.

Unless you are paddling the length of the inside passage you will probably arrive in this area by ferry or float plane and launch at either Bella Bella or Ocean Falls. From June to September ferries travel between Port Hardy on the north end of Vancouver Island and Prince Rupert, stopping at Bella Bella and Ocean Falls on only two days of the week, once on the northern trip and once on the southern trip. Foot passenger reservations are made with the British Columbia Ferry Corporation in Vancouver. The trip from Port Hardy to Bella Bella takes approximately 6½ hours. From Prince Rupert, it is a twelve hour voyage. Passengers and their gear must disembark at Bella Bella via a gangplank from the upper deck of the ship. Problem: How do you get a five metre fibreglass kayak from the car deck to the gangplank on the upper deck? Answer: Impossible. Launch directly into the sea from the ferry's car deck. This must be arranged in advance with the ship's crew. On the return journey the kayaks are loaded onto the ship via the gangplank and then lowered to the car deck when the ship berths at Port Hardy. You must have lines attached to both the bow and stern of your kayak to facilitate the loading and unloading procedure. As the ferry unloads cars at Ocean Falls it is easy to unload the kayak there. For those with folding kayaks, the Bella Bella area is accessible by scheduled float plane service on Air BC from Vancouver and Port Hardy and on Trans-Provincial Airlines from Prince Rupert.

Due to the expanse and diversity of the land and sea, we can provide just a sample of the sea kayaking experiences available in this unique wilderness. The choice of trip routes and the surprises along the way

North to Alaska!

are almost infinite. We recommend a circle route which gives you a taste of the distinct paddling environments in the area: the inside passage, the island lagoons, and the exposed outer islands. One of the best such circle routes starts at Bella Bella or Ocean Falls, proceeds along Seaforth Channel, then south through one of the lagoon-channels to Goose Island, then further south across Queens Sound to Calvert Island. The return north follows Fitz Hugh Sound, past the Koeye River and the village of Namu, to the departure point. The description which follows is based on this routing.

Bella Bella Village

In 1833 the Hudson's Bay Company established Fort McLoughlin and thereafter the settlement which is now known as Bella Bella, became the center of the dispersed Heiltsuk, or Bella Bella Indian nation. History gives this tribe a reputation for hostility. Alexander Mackenzie, who had trekked the overland route to the Pacific in 1793, scribbling a note to that affect on a rock in Elcho Harbour off Dean Channel fifty kilometres northeast of Bella Bella, was sent packing by the tribe. Today, New Bella Bella, which is directly across the channel from the old village site, is one of the largest Indian communities off British Columbia's mainland. It has all the facilities a kayaker needs, including a general store and pub. The Fisheries Officers stationed at the old village know the surrounding waters better than anyone else. Another small community is located further east in Shearwater Bay.

There are many Indian archeological sites near Bella Bella and the local Indians, if you gain their confidence, may direct you to some of these native treasures, such as a fine totem depicting a strikingly real human face topped by a four-tiered potlatch hat. A nearby burial island has many petroglyphs.

Ocean Falls

Ocean Falls is off most paddling routes and hence is a less desirable launching spot than more centrally located Bella Bella.

Over 3,000 people once lived in this company town. Recently a political decision closed the obsolete mill. The town died; just caretakers remain. White man's economy allows no permanent committment to this remote coastline. A store and pub services the skeleton community now.

Seaforth Channel

Seaforth Channel is just a few kilometres north of Bella Bella but is a two or three day paddle from Ocean Falls via Gunboat Passage. At the eastern end of Seaforth Channel on the southwest corner of Yeo Island, look for a fine rock carving. It will be found on the large shoreline boulder in front of the abandoned Indian village. This village, called Kilkite, was once one of the largest of the Bella Bella tribe. The early Hudson's Bay Company traders were loath to travel near it because of the ferocity of the villagers.

The Bella Bellas were great rock carvers. Every year new examples of their art are being discovered, many along Seaforth Channel and the adjoining passages. Ask at Bella Bella for further information. At Fisher Point on the northern shore of Seaforth Channel look for totem poles.

Island Lagoons

Lagoons open the interior of virtually every large island in the

Bella Bella area to the paddler. Two of the largest of these marine keyholes are just south of Seaforth Channel on both the west and east side of Athlone Island. Further south, there is another large lagoon penetrating the heart of Hunter Island: the Kildidt Lagoon. Tidal rapids guard the mouth of each of these lagoons. Navigable only during high slack, these obstacles preserve the sanctity of the inside waters.

Lagoons have an other-worldly ambiance. They are always peaceful and soft, even when the weather and the nearby sea are raging. The stunted forests along their edge seem to grow right out of the water, with no shoreline between. Finding flat ground on which to pitch a tent is often very difficult. The calls of geese, ducks, gulls, eagles and ospreys reverberate over these trapped seas. Their haunted music will echo in your mind long after the birds have departed.

Queens Sound

Because a thousand islets fringe Queens Sound, it is a particularly attractive area for paddlers. The waters can be dangerous, however.

Lagoon rapids between Athlone and Dufferin Islands

The North Coast

Tide rips and standing waves are common on the ebb tide at the mouths of the waterways which open onto the sound: Tide Rip Pass, Hunter Channel, Cultus Sound, Spider Channel.

On the northwest corner of Spider Island, near the lake, you will find the ruins of a World War II military base. A bush-covered road leads across the island to a gun emplacement facing the open ocean. With such a broad coast to defend, the gun's main value was symbolic. Just inside Spitfire Channel is a small float, usually ringed with trawlers sheltering from the open ocean. When we paddled in, the friendly fishermen there could not believe we had no "mother ship." They told us of a petroglyph on the west coast of Spitfire Island, but we could not find it. A few miles south, you may encounter geoduck (pronounced "gooey" duck) divers in Spider Anchorage. On a good day, these divers can earn $400.00 harvesting the giant clams, which are destined for chowder.

Goose Island

Of all the islands on the north coast, Goose Island stands out as the eccentric, and not just because it is the furthest out to sea. In every nook it hides a natural delight. The lagoon and tidal flats on its southern shore are clogged with shellfish and migratory birds. The sand beach on its northwestern coast, pulverized by the ocean surf, is the repository of Japanese glass balls, countless wooden or plastic floats, Japanese whiskey bottles, an old harpoon and the bones of its victim. Another arc of sand borders the protected north coast of the island. A stream trickles over each of the beaches, etching the sand with designs of great artistry. But the finest attribute of all is the belly of the island, a vast, almost surreal bogland. A photographer's paradise. A furry otter in a nest of crimson moss performs gentle surgery on a spiky purple urchin. Football fields away, a herd of deer nibbles on the undergrowth. The shoulder-high trees here are stooped and knarled in contrast to the massive evergreens which fringe the seashore.

Getting to this individualistic island involves five miles of open water paddling. Timing is vital. An early morning or evening crossing is best. If you approach Goose Island from the north, the McMullin Islets halfway across offer some protection.

Crossing Queens Sound from Goose Island south to Hunter or Calvert Island is a breathtaking ride in a sea kayak. To your right is the open Pacific Ocean; to your left the continent of North America. If the seas allow, somewhere in the middle of your voyage pull aboard your paddles and just float. It is the kayaker's equivalent to the mountain climber's pause at the top of a peak, a moment you will never forget.

Calvert Island

Calvert Island has two significant attractions: silver beaches and big spring salmon. The northwest coast of Calvert Island is a series of halfmoon beaches, strung tip to tip. A trail leads from a cabin at the west end of Kwakshua Channel across the neck of lowland to the ocean, passing two bizarre monsters cut into the trees by a chain saw sculptor. Only wolves and sports fishermen frequent the long sand beaches here. The exposed beach at mid-point on the west side of Calvert Island is an ecological reserve. Protected by the ocean, this beach is inviolable. To get here, paddlers must voyage along five miles of exposed coastline and then penetrate a barrier of surf.

The ocean swell is funnelled through Hakai Passage, but dissipates in Fitz Hugh Sound. The tide flows through Hakai Passage at four knots, towards the east on the flood, towards the west on the ebb. Nasty tide rips are created on the ocean side of Hakai Passage, especially near the north end of Calvert, when the west winds clash with the ebbing tide.

Fitz Hugh Sound

Approximately one third of the north coast inside passage twists through the islands surrounding Bella Bella. Much of it follows Fitz Hugh Sound where you can expect moderate ship traffic. It is a five mile paddle across Fitz Hugh Sound to the mainland from Calvert Island and its "hat," Hecate Island. A sunrise start is recommended for the crossing. We had to stop for an island-sized cruise ship plowing through the sound. A few passengers waved from its decks; how different were our perspectives.

Along this marine highway you may also cross paths with kayakers who, like the big ships, are plying the lengths of the inside passage. A surprising number of people, mostly from the United States, have paddled the route between the states of Washington and Alaska, and not just in kayaks. Dories, row boats and canoes have also been muscle-powered the distance. In our coastal travels we have met

Chain saw sculpture, Calvert Island   Photo: David John Smith

almost a dozen such adventurers. Curiously, only one of them had any kayak experience prior to undertaking the journey.

Koeye River

The Koeye River flows out of the mainland mountains into Fitz Hugh Sound. The broad sand beach will catch your eye from way out at sea. To paddle upriver is a marvellous detour. You will pass the ruins of the Koeye Lime Company, pass crumbling houses and their rusty contents scattered outside, pass jumping trout. A mile inland, the narrow river opens to a scene of unsurpassed beauty: a broad, grassy plain, a meandering river, a distant snow-capped peak. The sandy river bank captures the prints of a half dozen species: bear, wolf, river otter, racoon and waterfowl. You could easily spend a week exploring this very special watershed.

Namu

Archeological evidence indicates that man was hauling fish ashore at Namu 8,000 years ago. He still is today. The friendly outpost on the shores of Fitz Hugh Sound is the center of operations for a large trawler fleet.

It is interesting to watch the exchange of salmon at the packing company's dock, and hear of the success or failure of the fishermen. The public dock at Namu is often clogged with boats. The simultaneous comradeship and competitiveness of the fishermen is quickly evident here. After spending days alone at sea the fishermen come to Namu not just to deliver fish. A visit promises lively conversation, a shower and, on Saturday night, a movie. Sadly, the hardy trawler folk are an endangered species, like the fish they pursue.

Namu village is a network of boardwalks. They lead from the wharfs, past the store, liquor agency and well-tended little houses to the canteen (where meals are available) and further on to the native Indian village. A trail and boardwalk lead from the village to a fine sand beach on the shores of Namu Lake. Look for a petroglyph on the way.

From Namu you can return to either Bella Bella or Ocean Falls and take the ferry home. Air BC operates scheduled float plane service between Namu and Vancouver.

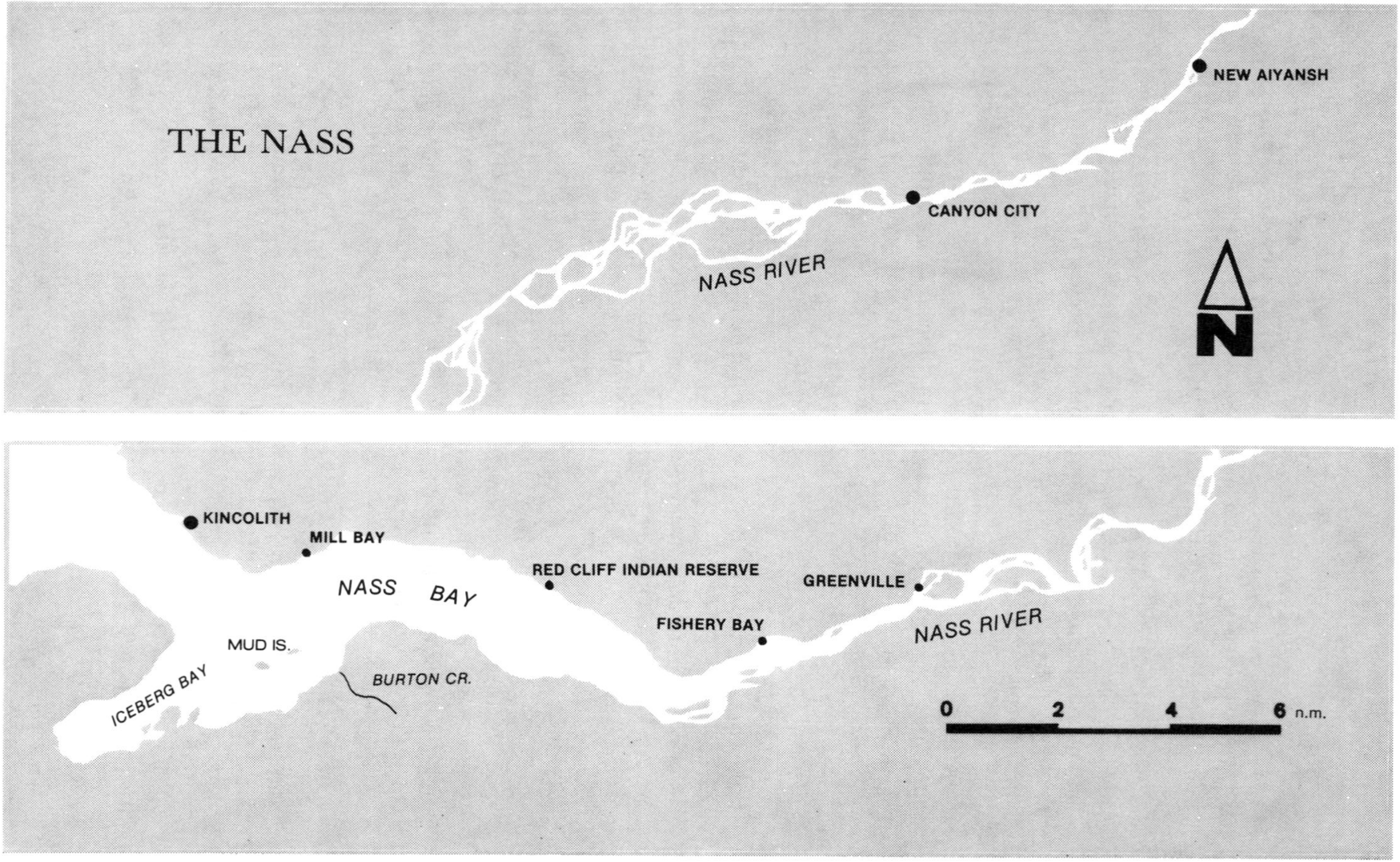

THE NASS

NEW AIYANSH

CANYON CITY

NASS RIVER

N

KINCOLITH

MILL BAY

NASS BAY

RED CLIFF INDIAN RESERVE

FISHERY BAY

GREENVILLE

NASS RIVER

BURTON CR.

MUD IS.

ICEBERG BAY

0   2   4   6 n.m.

The Nass

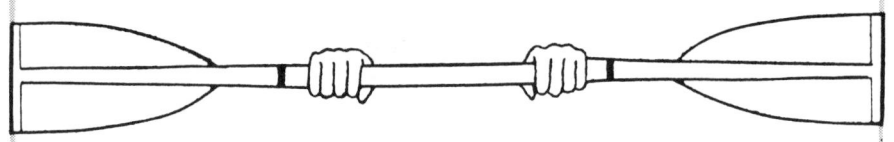

Area 13

Attractions: The phenomenal oolichan run. Vast swarms of birds. The extraordinary Nishga culture. A navigable river winding through lava beds. Hot springs.

Access: The Nass River valley is 105 km north of the town of Terrace. The villages along the river, New Aiyansh, Canyon City and Greenville, are accessible by logging road from Terrace. Kincolith, at the mouth of Nass Bay, is accessible by twice weekly British Columbia Ferry service and daily North Coast Air float plane service from Prince Rupert.

Seascape: Nass Bay: a shallow, largely protected waterbody, though susceptible to dangerous seas. Nass River: navigable from New Aiyansh to the sea. Some rapids between New Aiyansh and Canyon City.

Hazards: Nass Bay can be lethal when the outflowing ebb tide and river meet an inflowing wind over the shoals.

Season: March to October. For the oolichan run: first week in March to the first week in April.

Length: 3 to 7 days.

Camping: Winter camping during March and April; snow is not unusual.

Charts: 3790 Nass Bay	1:25,000
Nass River (National Topographic Series Maps):	
103I/13	1:50,000
103P/3	1:50,000
103P/4	1:50,000

The North Coast

Introduction

A paddling trip in March or early April in the waters of the Nass at the northern end of Canada's west coast promises to be rewarding. You will observe the legendary coastal oolichan run and the communal harvest of this fish by the Nishga Indians — a people who have maintained a traditional lifestyle unique in industrialized North America.

Every spring for thousands of years the Nishga have set up their fish camps at the mouth of the Nass River and taken tons of the smelt-like oolichan from the waters. Indicative of their dependence on and respect for these waters, the Indians named them "Nass" which means, literally, "the stomach." Perhaps the greatest reward of a paddling trip here is discovering the intimate bond that still exists between the Nishga and their river and sea.

While the early spring oolichan harvest is undeniably the main attraction, it is not the only reason to visit the Nass. The local people are friendly all year-round and the varied natural environment, consisting of lava beds, river rapids, canyons, marshes, mountains and sea, is pleasing in any season.

If you live in Prince Rupert, Kitimat or Terrace, the Nass is just a few hours drive away. From southern British Columbia, however, a road trip to the Nass is a major journey. From Vancouver, the Nass is 1462 kilometres by road, which is a very long drive, especially for a paddling trip that lasts just a week. Alternatively, you can reach Prince Rupert via ferry from either Vancouver or Port Hardy, depending on the season. The journey is much quicker and simpler by plane, but this option is only open to those with collapsible boats. CP Air has daily jet service to Terrace and Prince Rupert from Vancouver.

From just west of Terrace, a dirt road leads 197 kilometres to the Nass River valley. You can launch at the river near where the road forks to New Aiyansh, or at any number of spots downstream where the river and the road rub shoulders. The road ends at a log dump eight kilometres downstream from the village of Greenville, which is fifty kilometres west of New Aiyansh. We have had no trouble hitching a ride from Terrace up to the Nass, even when we were carrying two large bags and a five metre long kayak!

Your trip can begin in the sea rather than on the river. The British Columbia Ferry Corporation runs a passenger service twice a week to

Kincolith from Prince Rupert. No cars are carried but there is room on deck for kayaks. The ferry covers the distance in just three hours. Reservations are recommended. Contact either B.C. Ferries in Prince Rupert or the Indian band office in Kincolith. North Coast Air offers both charter and scheduled float plane service to Kincolith from Prince Rupert.

The Nishga Indians

The Nass valley is the ancestral homeland of the Nishga Indians, and today they claim much of this territory pursuant to their aboriginal title. Before visiting the Nass, it is prudent to discuss your paddling plans with the band manager in New Aiyansh.

The Nishga have one of the most interesting native communities in Canada. They have been in the forefront of the native rights movement and have established important legal precedents that affect all native people in Canada. They control their own schools, and their children are learning the native language. More significantly, they have retained many of their ageless traditions. The

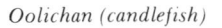

Oolichan (candlefish)

143

oolichan harvest and the art-science of oolichan oil production are still important cultural events. Slippery fish, dripping nets, and muscle power are a way of life for these people. The hard work gives no crisp pay cheque, but something they value much more: self-reliance in their homeland.

The Nishga feel that their lifestyle is seriously threatened by the daily dumping of tons of mine tailings from the Amax mine into Alice Arm, north of Nass Bay. The scientific reports provide no solace for the Nishga cannot believe that coating the sea bed with mine tailings poses no danger to their fishery. A Kincolith native summarized the conflict: "The mine is money, the sea is fish. White man lives on money, we on fish. Money won't take the risk, it will be the fish."

The Oolichan Harvest

The oolichan is such an oily fish that when held near a fire it will ignite and flame, which is why it is called the "candlefish." The oolichan spawn in many of the coastal inlets but the greatest oolichan fishery is at the doorstep of the Nishga in the mouth of the Nass.

In the past the oolichan harvest united the Nishga tribe in a common enterprise. Today the harvest has a similar unifying force, though mainly on a family rather than tribal basis. The oolichan has had important economic significance to the Nishga, who became wealthy trading the oil surplus with neighbouring tribes. Such a trade continues today, though on a much smaller scale than previously. The Nishga exchange the oil for seaweed, clams, oysters and other "Indian food."

From early March until the middle of April, you will see the fish camps in operation along the banks of Fishery Bay and further west in Nass Bay. When enough oolichan has been dried, smoked, salted or rendered into oil to fortify their kitchens for another year, the people return to their villages.

Like hundreds of mirrors, the silvery oolichan reflect the sun as they are emptied from conical-shaped nets into river boats and then transported to huge wooden vats on shore. Men excavate clay from the riverbed to line the burning pits underneath the oolichan vats and saw logs into slabs which will be hauled to the pits to provide fuel for the eighteen-hour fire. The oil so rendered is a rich, non-fishy tasting

Oolichan drying racks

Fishery Bay, 1903   *Photo: Courtesy of the British Columbia Provincial Museum, Victoria, British Columbia*

delicacy. Sun-drying racks made from freshly debarked cedar poles project five metres into the air, like a giant's tripod. The women of the camp deftly twist pairs of oolichan onto specially prepared cedar strips which are then strung on the drying racks. Nearby, a sea lion flipper is broiled over an open fire in preparation for a feast.

The oolichan run is an event that attracts not only the human species. Clouds of birds — mostly gulls — descend on the river. Their shrill chorus echoes between the mountains. Dozens of oolichan-fed, pot-bellied eagles ornament the shoreline trees. Paddlers will be entertained (and splashed) by the great numbers of seals and sea lions stalking the oolichan.

Nass River

In March, snow frequently covers the ground and ice the river. Determine the weather conditions here before you leave home. Being so far north, you can count on twelve hours of daylight. Near New Aiyansh, the river flows past square kilometres of the Tseax lava bed. It is almost impossible to walk on this mass of sharp-edged rocks, but a short hike reveals wild lava sculptures, shadowy crevices and colourful lichens — life's first attempt to reclaim the barren wasteland.

The river will whisk the paddler downstream, a new adventure for sea kayakers. You may have to negotiate rapids between New Aiyansh and Canyon City. At Canyon City ask the residents to point out the petroglyph on the river bank. Avoid the Indian fishing nets in the river.

Greenville has a store and a horde of inquisitive kids. Below Greenville the tidal flow is as important as the river current. Beyond Fishery Bay, especially at low tide, you must keep to the channel that nature has carved through the sand flats. The National Topographic Series Maps indicate the location of the sandbars which obstruct the river. Past Fishery Bay, at the Red Cliff Indian Reserve, you will find more fish camps; these are operated by the Tsimshian Indians from Port Simpson, a village south of the Nass. The snow-freckled mountains rise suddenly as you get closer to the sea. The narrow scar, caused by the powerline on the north coast of the bay is nothing compared to the planned clear-cut logging of the slopes behind, scheduled to begin in 1984.

Nass Bay

Nass Bay can be dangerous. When the winds slam out of Iceberg Bay over the Nass Bay shoals and collide with the ebbing tide and river current, watch out! We got caught in a series of standing waves here that were almost impossible to navigate. Luck and perseverance got us through these liquid pyramids.

Before the turn of the century a cannery operated at Mill Bay. Rusting fuel tanks, a thicket of rotten piles and heaps of collapsed buildings are the only remains. Look for a hot spring near Burton Creek, due east of the Mud Islands. Follow the rough trail on the north side of the creek. Where the trail ends you will find the hot spring bubbling out of a small stream.

Kincolith, meaning "place of the scalps," has known better days. Before the road was pushed through to Aiyansh, Kincolith was the main Nishga community, an entrepot for freight shipped in and out of the Nass. The elegant design of the church and stately houses remind you of Kincolith's former ascendancy. Today, it has a dreary aspect with many fire-gutted structures and piles of litter.

Oolichan fisherman

The Kincolith natives relish sea lion meat. On a beach near Kincolith we found the long bloody spine of a recently butchered sea lion, a gull feeding on each disc. The voluminous entrails of the beast, a colourful mass, lay a short distance away. We watched the women of Kincolith cut the meat on large tables outside their homes. After their work they treated us to a very tasty sea lion stew.

Kincolith has a hotel and cafe, located in the band council buildings, and a store. The ferry to Prince Rupert docks at the government wharf, one mile west of the town.

West coast elements: fog and swell

Chapter Eight
THE WEST COAST OF VANCOUVER ISLAND

The Pacific Ocean. An endless golden beach. The mighty flukes of a grey whale. The setting sun engulfing the horizon in flame. This is the west coast of Vancouver Island. A sea kayaker's extravaganza.

This chapter examines the entire length of the island's outer coast, with two exceptions: the Long Beach area, which, with its heavy surf and National Park camping restrictions, is suitable only for weekend surfing fun, and the West Coast Trail leg of the Pacific Rim National Park between Bamfield and Port Renfrew, a long, unprotected coastline, very popular with hikers.

Though there are very many stretches of coastline exposed to the ocean, only at a few areas is it difficult to find a sheltered landing spot, thanks to the numerous inlets and sounds which indent the west coast of Vancouver Island. To traverse the open coastline you or someone in your group must have previous ocean paddling experience. Solo kayakers or those new to ocean paddling can set up base camp in the protected inlets and sounds and explore the open ocean on day excursions. Each of the areas discussed in this chapter is accessible from a road-end launching site adjacent to sheltered waters.

It is widely believed that the sun never shines on the west coast of Vancouver Island. In fact, statistics show that on average, two thirds of the days in July and August are completely dry. In two summers, we spent a total of eight weeks on this coast and only for one day did the rain confine us to our tents. In the summer, the fog is likely to be more bothersome than the rain. The fog can persist for days along this coast.

The west coast of Vancouver Island has a fascinating history, and it is etched along the shoreline in Indian middens, totem poles, shipwrecks and abandoned villages. For an entertaining history, see *Vancouver Island's West Coast 1762-1962* by George Nicholson.

VANCOUVER ISLAND

TOQUART
BAY   HILLIER IS.

PIPESTEM INLET

THE BROKEN ISLANDS

0   1   2
n.m.

STOPPER
ISLANDS

N

PINKERTON
ISLANDS

HAND IS.

JULIA
PASSAGE

BRABANT ISLANDS

NETTLE IS.

JARVIS IS.

SWALE ROCK ·

DODD IS.

JACQUES IS.

WILLIS IS.

GIBRALTAR IS.

LOUDOUN CHANNEL

TURTLE IS.

DEMPSTER IS.

TURRET IS.

CLARKE IS.

BENSON IS.

COASTER CHANNEL

GILBERT IS.

IMPERIAL EAGLE CHANNEL

EFFINGHAM IS.

DICEBOX IS.

Meares Bluff

WOUWER IS.

AUSTIN IS.

☒ = CAMPING

BARKLEY   SOUND

The Broken Islands

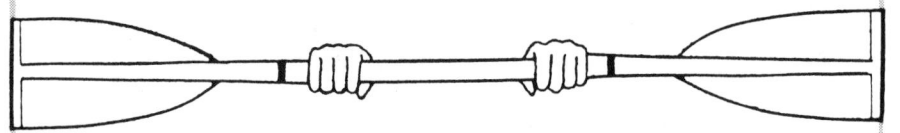

Area 14

Attractions: A cluster of picturesque islands in sheltered waters, yet with the open ocean nearby. Perfect for family paddling. Rich intertidal life. Many sea caves. Prime sea bird habitat.

Access: Drive to the town of Port Alberni on Vancouver Island and take the passenger vessel *M.V. Lady Rose* directly to the Broken Group. Or launch at Toquart Bay. From Port Alberni follow Highway 4 west for 88 km. As you drive past the edge of Kennedy Lake look to your left for a logging road. Follow the logging road to Toquart Bay.

Seascape: Within the Broken Group the sea is generally quiet, as the outer islands diminish the force of the Pacific winds and swell. Short crossings. Swell and surge in the outer islands. Outside the Broken Group, the channels are unprotected and the crossings exceed 3 miles.

Hazards: The anchorages in the Broken Group can be congested with speedboats, sailboats, trawlers and dive charters. Crossings from Bamfield or Ucluelet are suitable only for experienced sea kayakers.

Season: April to October. Crowded in July and August.

Length: 3 to 10 days.

Camping: The Broken Group is within the Pacific Rim National Park. Camping is permitted only at designated sites. Drinking water may become scarce during extended dry periods.

Charts: 3671 Barkley Sound   1:40,000
            3638 Broken Group (Barkley Sound)   1:18,200

West Coast - Vancouver Island

Introduction

The Broken Group has become a mecca for sea kayakers and sea canoeists, especially for those new to the sport and those with children. This scenic array of islands, isolated from Vancouver Island by expansive Barkley Sound and face to face with the open ocean, has the wild ruggedness of an exposed coastline. The islands enclose protected waterways that pose little threat to the inexperienced paddler.

The Broken Group is within the boundaries of the Pacific Rim National Park with consequent advantages and disadvantages to sea kayakers and canoeists. On the positive side, the park status ensures that the islands will be preserved in their natural state in perpetuity. On the negative side, the park regulations allow visitors to camp only at seven locations, and in the summer season these are crowded, often very crowded. Although Parks Canada lacks the personnel to strictly enforce the regulations, the wardens will expel anyone found camping outside a designated site. It can be a bother to camp only at selected locations, especially if the neighbours are noisy, but the heavy use of the islands make the camping restrictions a necessity. In the summer, the Broken Islands are only recommended if you are gregarious and want to meet other paddlers. Before June or after September you can expect to tour the islands virtually alone.

The easiest and most enjoyable way to reach the Broken Islands is via the *M.V. Lady Rose*, based in Port Alberni. This small freighter, operated by Alberni Marine Transportation Ltd., delivers kayakers, canoeists and their boats from Port Alberni or Ucluelet to the float near Gibraltar Island at the southeast corner of the Broken Group. Contact the operator to determine the current schedule and to reserve deck space for your kayak or canoe. The 60-kilometre trip from Port Alberni takes three hours and follows the Alberni Inlet, a long sliver of a waterway that almost bisects Vancouver Island.

If you launch at Toquart Bay, a five mile paddle through largely protected waters will take you to the Broken Group. During the summer the scene at Toquart Bay is quite bizzare. Scores of recreational vehicles are packed together along the sandy beach like driftwood after a storm. There are so many people here it could be Waikiki. Unattended cars have been vandalized.

Toquart Bay to Stopper Islands

Named after the Toquaht tribe which inhabited the area, Toquart Bay has for over a century bustled with commerce and industry. The early traders established a trading post on Hillier Island in the 1850's. The mountains near Toquart Bay show the effects of past and present logging. In the 1960's Toquart Bay became the port for the nearby iron ore mine. During the seven year life of the mine, five million tons of ore were shipped to Japan.

To the east, Pipestem Inlet is a veritable gorge. From this waterbody, which in certain places is only a few boat-lengths wide, the mountains rise suddenly to heights exceeding 1000 metres.

The primeval rain forests on the Stopper Islands are worth a visit, especially after the summertime suburbia ot Toquart Bay. One wonders how the massive timber here escaped the saw. To walk far in this west coast jungle is very difficult: just peering into it is reward enough. Leaving the Stopper Islands, look back to the mountain range behind Toquart Bay for the profile of the "sleeping warrior."

Pinkerton Islands to Julia Passage

The Pinkerton Group outside the National Park boundaries is a delightful weave of tiny islands and street-width waterways. It is the Broken Group in miniature. Bugs are not a problem in the Broken Group, but along the shore adjacent to the Pinkerton Group they are nasty. In Julia Passage, the houseboats demonstrate that land is not an essential pre-requisite for a home in the wilderness.

In 1787 Captain Charles Barkley, a 25-year-old fur trader, became the first white person to explore these waters. He is responsible for many of the names which now appear on the chart. Imperial Eagle Channel was named after his ship. At the northern end of this channel, one mile offshore from Julia Passage, are the Baeria Rocks. Pelagic cormorants, gulls and pigeon guillemots nest here. Like many other reefs in Barkley Sound, the Baeria Rocks are popular with divers, due to the varied and colourful marine life. You do not have to go underwater to enjoy this visual smorgasbord. Just sit beside one of the many tidal pools and peer down. The marine and sea bird habitat of the Baeria Rocks are within an ecological reserve.

Wilderness floating home

Broken Islands: Island Harbour Group

Jacques Island encloses the largest lagoon in the Broken Group. It is a spooky place: the water is thick with eelgrass and moss hangs from the trees like curtains. Bird lovers could spend many happy hours in this lagoon. The Broken Group has over two hundred species of birds and many wing and whistle over the lagoon's placid waters. At the southwest corner of the lagoon, in the opening between Jarvis Island and Jacques Island, look for the remains of an ancient Indian fish trap. At high tide the fish would swim into the pits, and when the water receded they could not escape.

The float at Gibraltar island is frequently crowded with pleasure boats. If the *Lady Rose* cannot dock at the float, kayakers will be launched from the ship directly into the water. Gibraltar has a good freshwater spring near the camping area.

Look for the large sea caves on the southwest side of Dempster Island. The southern-most cave is the largest and you can actually paddle into its blackness. To the north, listen for a blowhole cave. The ocean surge is its powerful "lungs." Birds nest in the caves and may flap in the face of an intruder.

The park warden's cabin is situated on Nettle Island, on the east side of the large bay. The best fishing spot in the Broken Group is just east of Nettle Island at Swale Rock.

Broken Group: Hand Island to Turtle Island

Hand Island is the closest of the Broken Group to Toquart Bay. Its three white beaches are excellent for camping. The grass field nearby was once the site of a trading post. Potable water used to be available on the island, but is no longer, as the well has been vandalized. The Brabant Islands are named after a Roman Catholic missionary who lived amongst the natives of the west coast of Vancouver Island between 1869 and 1910. Native paddlers often ferried Father Brabant across the fifteen mile wide mouth of Barkley Sound in a dugout canoe, a voyage modern paddlers can well respect. The history books reveal that many such paddling expeditions across the wide, unprotected channels which border the Broken Group, ended in grief.

Turtle Island was for years the home of "Salal Joe." His garden was located atop an Indian midden on Dodd Island. The federal government allowed the hermit to live on Turtle Island even after it

Hand Island

was included in the National Park. Sadly, Salal Joe disappeared in 1980 and it is believed that Barkley Sound claimed another victim. The lagoon north of Turtle Island is a popular anchorage for yachts.

Broken Group: Outer Islands

The ocean swell undulates through the water surrounding the southern-most islands of the Broken Group. Clarke Island with its float, camping area, cabin and water supply is a crowded spot in the summer. Nearby, Benson Island — it too has a camping site with water — has been receiving visitors for over 90 years. In 1893, John Benson built a hotel and planted a garden and orchard to supply it. Traces of the enterprise can still be seen. From Benson Island, it is an eight mile open water paddle across Loudoun Channel to the village of Ucluelet. Do not attempt this crossing unless you are an experienced ocean paddler.

On a calm day, paddlers can head out Coaster Channel and into the Pacific Ocean, thereby getting acquainted with ocean swell. Sea lions lay their blubbery bodies atop the outside islets and rocks. See especially the islets southwest of Wouwer Island. You can smell and hear the beasts from a great distance. Treat the growling, self-important bulls with respect, as they are extremely territorial. You will need a telephoto lens to get the animals within camera range. The surge will keep you away from the rocks, and you should stay clear of the rookeries in any case. Jumping into the water, the animals can easily capsize a small craft. One fisherman was crushed to death when a sea lion landed on him.

Tiny Dicebox Island has two fine caves near its southwest tip. The first is like a tunnel. Dry except at high tide, it opens onto two sides of the island. Further east, a cave shaft penetrates into the island, well above the tide line. A short walk into the cave and you will discover miniature stalactites. Do not touch them as it stunts their growth. Bring a flashlight.

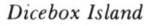

Dicebox Island

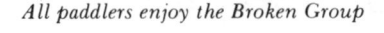

All paddlers enjoy the Broken Group

160

Barkley Sound is so wide that deep-sea skippers frequently confuse it for Juan de Fuca Strait, discovering their error atop a deadly reef. Due to the numbers of ships they have sent to the bottom, Barkley Sound and the coastline south of it have earned the title "graveyard of the Pacific." In 1972, the Japanese freighter *Vanlene* struck the rocks off Austin Island and sank with a full load of new cars. For further information see *Shipwrecks of British Columbia* by Fred Rogers.

On Effingham Island, Meares Bluff is worth exploring. A number of sea caves are scooped into the island near the shoreline. Fins and feathers are thick along the bluffs. Above the water line a great number of cormorants nest in rocky ledges. The bluffs plummet underwater and here salmon and red snapper regularly make fatal meal selections, much to the enjoyment of hook-tugging fishermen.

If you are adventurous, consider the 3½ mile excursion across Imperial Eagle Channel to the Deer Islands, and then on to the village of Bamfield and Cape Beale. Bamfield is the terminus of the submarine cable from Australia. The lighthouse at Cape Beale is one of the most important on Canada's west coast, guiding ocean-going vessels in and out of Juan de Fuca Strait.

VANCOUVER ISLAND

MEGIN RIVER

OBSTRUCTION IS.

INLET

SHELTER

SIDNEY

INLET

BEDWELL SOUND

HERBERT INLET

MILLAR CHANNEL

Catface Range

MEARES IS.

ADVENTURE COVE

LEMMENS INLET

RITCHIE B.

Lone Cone

CHETARPE

MARKTOSIS

MATILDA INLET

SULPHUR SPRINGS

WHITESAND COVE

WHALER IT.

BURGESS IS.

BARTLETT IS.

KAKAWIS

OPITSAT

STUBBS IS.

TOFINO

WICKANINNISH IS.

VARGAS ISLAND

LA CROIX GROUP

AHOUS B.

Ahous Pt.

FLORES ISLAND

HOT SPRINGS COVE

HOT SPRINGS

Sharp Pt.

COW CR.

Rafael Pt.

CLAYOQUOT

SOUND

HESQUIAT HARBOUR

HESQUIAT BAR

HESQUIAT

Matlahaw Point

Hesquiat Peninsula

HOMAIS COVE

Estevan Point

BOAT BASIN

N

PACIFIC OCEAN

CLAYOQUOT SOUND

| 0 | 2 | 4 | 6 | 8 n.m. |

Clayoquot Sound

Area 15

Attractions: A multi-tiered hot spring steaming down to the sea. Friendly sea mammoths: grey whales, basking sharks, sea lions. Abundant bird life. Virgin rain forests and golden beaches.

Access: Drive to the town of Tofino at the terminus of Highway 4 on the west coast of Vancouver Island. Launch at the public wharf or the adjacent beach.

Seascape: Two options: sheltered, usually calm inside passage or exposed ocean. A circle route takes the paddler through both.

Hazards: The waters off Tofino are heavily travelled by boats and float planes. The currents, winds and shoals here can give the paddler a rough ride. Swell, heavy surf and fog are common on the exposed coast route.

Season: April to October. Expect a crowd at the hot spring on virtually any weekend.

Length: 6 to 12 days.

Camping: Beaches everywhere, so camping is no problem, although most of the outer beaches are usually accessible only through surf.

Charts: 3640 Clayoquot Sound, Lennard Island to
Estevan Point — 1:77,500
3648 Clayoquot Sound (Northwest Portion) — 1:36,500
3649 Clayoquot Sound (Southeast Portion) — 1:40,000

Introduction

The trip from Tofino to Hot Springs Cove and back is fast becoming one of the most popular on the coast. It is easy to understand why. The natural environment is enchanting. The mountains are shaped like volcanoes and you almost expect a belch of smoke from the top of these huge cones. The land frequently greets the sea with a golden smile — a curving sandy beach. Gentle underwater monsters haunt the sea, breaking the surface to display their geometric anatomy: the delta flukes of a grey whale, the triangular fin of a basking shark. And in the midst of all this, a hot spring boiling out of a rocky peninsula and spilling down through a series of natural pools into the sea.

You can paddle to Hot Springs Cove via either side of Vargas and Flores Islands. The east coast, preferred by kayakers unfamiliar with open ocean kayaking and by all paddlers during storms, is longer and generally less interesting than the outer coast route. If the weather is favourable at the start of the trip, take the outside route to Hot Springs Cove, leaving the inside passage as a return option. Flores and Vargas block the ocean swell from the inside passage, but wind and tidal currents can create choppy waters. Between the two islands, beneath the Catface Range, is a four-mile stretch of exposed coast.

Most of the Clayoquot Sound area is surprisingly unspoiled. Few of the mountain slopes have been shaved. The security of the forest is likely short-term, however. Fallers have been busy on Meares Island. A conservation group in Tofino, the Friends of Clayoquot, is trying to halt further logging there. Vargas Island is a tree farm and patches of the forests on Flores have already felt the bite of a chain saw.

Though it is not unusual to see other paddlers along the route, it is easy to be alone in this rugged territory. Except at Hot Springs Cove. Fishermen and native Indians who have bathed and showered in the hot spring for decades are now outnumbered in the summer season by the hordes of fly-in campers, pleasure boaters and paddlers who go to the hot spring for a soak. Especially on summer weekends, expect a social soak.

Launch at the public wharf at Tofino (do not launch from the sea plane float on the right side), or at the beach nearby. The pilots here are usually generous with the latest weather information. To avoid vandalism do not leave your vehicle parked for the duration of the trip near the Maquinna Hotel. Inquire at the Canada Fisheries office in Tofino regarding the red tide. Be sure to fill water containers, as drinking water is difficult to get on the outer route.

Paddlers who want to explore Meares Island and its protected surrounding waters can launch at Grice Bay. Watch for the turnoff thirteen kilometres south of Tofino.

Tofino Area

Tofino is a charming village. Fishermen, artists, tourists, Indians, loggers, pilots and bureaucrats — the personalities here are colourful and most of them seem to visit the government dock.

The sandy spit on Stubbs Island, a half mile north of Tofino, was once a grim landmark. After vanquishing the Kyuquot tribe in 1855, in the last battle fought between natives on the coast, the Clayoquots beheaded eighteen victims and displayed the trophies atop poles on the spit. For years, passing mariners observed these macabre sentinels. Today, a lodge operates on the island and serves tasty meals. Splurging there for dinner is a fine way to end a trip.

At Wickaninnish Island, named after the great Clayoquot chief, the natives skirmished with the American fur-trading ship *Tonquin* in 1811. Thanks to the fur trade, the richly-furred sea otter which inhabited the west coast of Vancouver Island was exterminated. So were the crew members of the *Tonquin*. A mysterious explosion sunk the ship.

Meares Island

Kayakers pass Meares Island on their way to or from Hot Springs Cove, but rarely explore it. The eelgrass flats of Lemmens Inlet and Ritchie Bay are among the most important resting places for migratory birds on the Pacific coast. Oysters, clams and crabs abound. Salmon spawn in many streams, and the island is almost surrounded by herring spawning beds. It is not surprising that the shoreline of Meares Island, so rich in protein, is lined with Indian middens.

In 1791 Robert Gray, an American trader who was one of the first white men to winter on the west coast, built Fort Defiance and a small schooner, the *Adventure*, at Adventure Cove in Lemmens Inlet. The fort site has been designated a British Columbia Historic Site.

Two important Indian communities are located on Meares Island. The houses of Opitsat are visible from Tofino, and the Opitsat

Kelp anchor

residents regularly travel back and forth by water taxi. Kakawis, at the base of Lone Cone, was formerly the location of a large Roman Catholic residential school. Its tall cross is still a landmark. The Kakawis Family Development Centre now occupies the buildings of the former school. This residential program is aimed primarily at rehabilitating those suffering from alcoholism.

Vargas Island

Flat Vargas Island is the most beach-endowed island on Canada's west coast. It is almost ringed with sand. The La Croix Group off the southwest coast of Vargas Island is popular with sports fishermen. We tried our luck there, and in a twenty-minute troll we hooked four coho. An Indian village was once located at Ahous Point, but nothing remains. Ahous Bay is a favourite snack bar for grey whales. The paddler can get close enough to see the barnacles which adhere to the long backs of the spray-spouting beasts. Occasionally the animals will pirouette out of the water and then splash back like a dropped bomb — something we were happy to observe from a distance.

The surf smacks Ahous Bay with ferocity. Paddlers can avoid it by tucking behind the rocky fingers that extend from either end of the bay. The surf on the northwest corner of the island, opposite Burgess Island, is milder. One of the very few streams on the island trickles onto the shore here. The small islands to the north and west of Vargas are colonized by large numbers of birds, notably storm petrels, pigeon guillemots, and rhinoceros auklets, the latter distinguished by a strange protrusion that grows above their beaks. Whaler Islet, east of Bartlett Island, is a sand dune in the middle of the sea — an excellent lunch-stop.

North of Vargas, below the Catface Range on Vancouver Island, you will find squatters' homes tucked into the foliage; some are finely crafted with turrets and domes. There are few traces of the charted settlement at Chetarpe.

Flores Island

The virgin beauty of the west side of Flores Island is striking. Between Marktosis and Rafael Point lies an almost continous band of golden sand beach. Behind, the slopes rise gently from the shoreline and are dense with timber. The mountain tops ripple the skyline with a series of knobs and cones. It would be a pity to miss this coast, but as it directly abuts the open ocean, it is often too wild for paddlers. The reefs and shoals offshore deserve respect even on calm days. The reefs are forested with sea palms which look like miniatures of the tropical tree. They thrive only in perpetual surf. Shipwrecks are piled on top of each other in the depths near Rafael Point.

A few squatters' huts dot the beaches on Flores. Cow Creek is one of the few charted streams on the outside route, and large numbers of paddlers stop there for water. The small group of people living next to the creek, who settled on this rugged coastline in search of solitude, have come to loathe kayakers, and openly admit it. They do not want visitors.

Marktosis is the modern village of the Ahousat Band on the southeast corner of the island, and paddlers can stock up at the store. Some of the elders in the village tell entertaining stories about their youthful life. North of Marktosis is the Ahousat cemetery. Brightly-coloured plastic flowers decorate the graves, along with some possessions of the deceased: a baseball cap, a mug, a rusty sewing machine.

167

Chart 3640 indicates the location of the Ahousat sulphur springs at the head of Matilda Inlet. The springs are lukewarm. There are three ways of getting to them. First, by a rough trail leading from Marktosis to the mud flats at the end of the inlet. At low tide you can walk over the flats to the springs. At high tide, follow the shoreline. Secondly, you can paddle directly to the springs via Matilda Inlet, keeping to the west of the island at the head of the inlet. The final alternative is to paddle to Whitesand Cove and take the well-cut trail across to the springs. A cement pool, set into a grassy bank, collects the springwater. The water is clear and drinkable. The springs, trail and white sand beach are within the boundaries of the Gibson Marine Park.

Shelter Inlet

Large patches of Vancouver Island across from Flores Island have been logged. We stopped for lunch at a beach here and a black bear sauntered out of the woods, no doubt intending to join in the meal. It is quite common to see basking sharks lazing about in the water here. Among the largest of the shark family, these creatures eat only plankton. They are hated by fishermen as they often get fouled in the fishing nets. Obstruction Island, off the northeast corner of Flores Island, was the site of one of the largest drug busts in Canadian history. A ship allegedly carrying a cargo of marijuana was apprehended here. Directly north of Obstruction Island, navigate the Megin River for some excellent trout fishing. Good camping spots are scarce in Shelter Inlet.

Hot Springs Cove

No kayak trip could have a more pleasing destination than Hot Springs Cove. Situated at the end of the Openit Peninsula, the springs sluice out of a rocky outcropping and spill over a ledge, making a perfect shower. The steaming water fills numerous split-level pools, huge natural bath tubs, which, depending on the level of the tide, are alternately hot and cool, according to the pulse of the sea. Soaking in this soothing sulphur liquid, facing the setting sun, savouring the thick aroma of the ocean, a mug of wine at hand — this is sensual bliss. Because the delights of Hot Springs Cove are widely known, it is difficult to enjoy them alone. It is an interesting social experience to be amongst a crowd of strangers mingling at

Hot Springs Cove

close quarters in various stages of undress.

The hot springs are within the Maquinna Provincial Park. There are few flat spots close to the springs, and in any case camping here is undesirable on a summer weekend due to the heavy pedestrian traffic. It is possible to land kayaks on both sides of the peninsula near the springs, but the surge makes this difficult, especially on the west side.

From the public wharf in Hot Springs Cove, a boardwalk trail leads 1.2 miles through a lush rain forest to the hot springs. In the summer, fishing boats and yachts, sometimes rafted together in pairs or triplets, hug all sides of the dock. A store, fish buying station, school and post office, which once existed here, are now just derelict buildings.

Drinking water is difficult to find in Hot Springs Cove. Many believe in the curative powers of the mineral-rich hot springs. Look for fresh water at the north end of the beach across the cove from the dock. You must walk into the bush to find the tiny stream. The fishermen and pleasure boaters at the dock usually can spare a few litres of drinking water.

The foghorn and light at Sharp Point are notable, as they are powered by the nearby windmill. In 1964, Hot Springs Cove funnelled in the seismic tidal wave that had been triggered by the Alaskan earthquake. Many Indians living at the village at the head of the cove lost their homes.

Hesquiat Peninsula

Ten miles northwest of Hot Springs Cove lies the curiously flat Hesquiat Peninsula. For almost two centuries mariners have travelled around this exposed peninsula with great caution. The route from Hot Springs Cove to Hesquiat, and then around Estevan Point up to Nootka Island is completely unprotected, and the underwater ledge of the peninsula, combined with the strong tidal flow and the wind, swell and fog, can be dangerous. Hesquiat Harbour is somewhat protected, but crossing the Hesquiat Bar is treacherous in heavy seas. Only advanced sea kayakers should explore this area.

The first Christian mission on the west coast of Vancouver Island was established at Hesquiat in 1875. There were numerous attempts to farm the area, but these proved unsuccessful. Wild cows, decendants of the herds brought here over sixty years ago, are still spotted in the bush. Today only one family lives at Hesquiat village. Just west of Matlahaw Point, on one of the large foreshore boulders, look for an Indian petroglyph. Along the coastline between Hesquiat and Hot Springs Cove, you might still find traces of a land route known as "Smugglers' Trail."

There are many burial caves along the shoreline of Hesquiat Harbour. The contents of these caves have been studied by a team of archeologists. The scientists found that a Hesquiat native had a life expectancy of only 21.6 years. Due to the vandalism, the Hesquiat Band has removed all of the cultural items and skeletal remains from the caves. If you want to visit the caves, the band may indicate their precise location.

A trail connects Hesquiat with the lighthouse at Estevan Point, the tallest on Vancouver Island, and proceeds further north to the abandoned native village site at Homais Cove. The first white man to explore Canada's west coast, Captain Juan Perez, made contact with the Hesquiat natives in the waters off Estevan Point in 1774 — four years before Captain Cook set foot on Nootka Island. Estevan Point made the history books again when, in 1942, a Japanese submarine lobbed over twenty shells at the lighthouse, doing little damage. Some of the missiles flew right over the peninsula, landing near the Hesquiat village. This was the only time Canada was attacked in World War II.

Surf riders

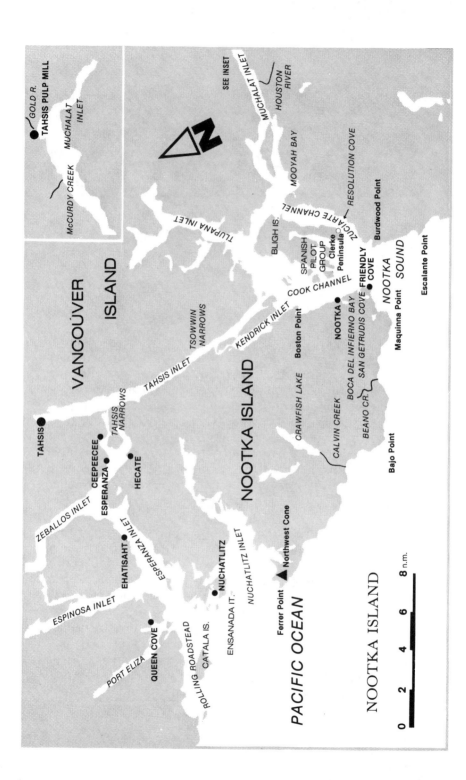

Nootka Island

Area 16

Attractions: Historically fascinating: great explorers and Indian chiefs, colonial soldiers and fur traders once walked these desolate shores. Forsaken Indian villages. Two of the finest totem poles on the coast. Remote, open ocean paddling.

Access: Drive past the town of Gold River, which is 92 km east of Campbell River on Highway 28, to the pulp mill at the head of Muchalat Inlet. Launch at the public wharf or from the banks of the Gold River. Or take the *M.V. Uchuck III* to Friendly Cove or to any of a number of points along the ship's route. Paddle back to the car or return with the *Uchuck III*.

Seascape: Open ocean on the west side of Nootka Island. Long, narrow inlets on the lee side. Two-mile crossings to Nootka Island across the mouth of Nootka Sound in the south, and Esperanza Inlet in the north.

Hazards: The entire open ocean coast is subject to heavy swell and fog. Watch for reefs at Bajo Point and at the mouth of Esperanza Inlet. Small craft can be buffeted by the chop in Muchalat Inlet.

Season: April to October. Driest in July and August. Never crowded.

Length: 5 to 14 days; 5 days if the trip is restricted to one area, such as Friendly Cove or Nuchatlitz; 2 weeks if circumnavigating Nootka Island.

Camping: At abandoned logging camps along the inside route. Beach camping on the exposed coast.

Charts: 3662 Nootka Sound to Esperanza Inlet   1:75,000
        3663 Esperanza Inlet   1:40,000
        3664 Nootka Sound   1:40,000

Introduction

To paddle the waters surrounding Nootka Island is to explore history as much as geography. Here the coast's first white visitors stepped ashore over 200 years ago. Later, the Spanish and the British empires almost battled over this isolated piece of real estate. In scores of now-abandoned villages, the Nootka natives skillfully lived off the sea. Traces of the cultures which accidentally converged here are still visible.

Though the Vancouver Island mountains to the north and northeast of Nootka Island are impressive, and the inlets are like gorges, the scenery here reveals massive logging scars. Only on the northwest and south coasts of Nootka Island and along the lowlands of Escalante are the forests not clipped. But then the prime attraction is not the wilderness, but the story of man's relationship to it.

If you plan to take the *Uchuck III*, contact its operators, Nootka Sound Service Ltd. before leaving home to determine the current schedule of the freighter service. It is also possible to launch from the two mill towns of Tahsis or Zeballos, north of Nootka Island. However, both are accessible only by rough logging roads and the driving time is much longer than to Gold River.

Muchalat Inlet

Named after the local Indian tribe, Muchalat Inlet is similar to the long, narrow waterways that jab the mainland of British Columbia. There are many fine cliffs along the inlet, and for most of its length the sheer mountains form right angles with the water. The mouth of the Gold River is a very popular recreational salmon fishing spot.

Camping along the inlet is restricted to the shoreline remains of old logging operations and the deltas of the major streams that tumble down from the heights. Active logging camps are located at McCurdy Creek, Houston River and Mooyah Bay.

If you take the *Uchuck III* from Gold River, consider paddling back. In the summer the prevailing winds blow from west to east, mainly in the afternoon. Local fishermen warned us about the chop in Muchalat Inlet. The waterway funnels both the wind and tide, and when they run into each other, the sea can be rough. We covered 23 miles from Friendly Cove to Gold River easily in one day, wind and tide in our favour.

Bligh Island

Bligh Island, at the mouth of Muchalat Inlet, is named after the infamous Captain Bligh, who sailed these waters with Captain Cook before gaining notoriety on the *Bounty*. At Resolution Cove, on the southeast corner of the island, Captain Cook started the west coast's greatest industry, chopping a tree for use as a mast on his ship, *H.M.S. Resolution*. A cairn there commemorates the event. Near Resolution Cove we paddled through patches of water that seemed to be bloodied, as if a whale had been slaughtered. In fact, it was the red tide.

Look for the hulk of the charted shipwreck in Zuciarte Channel, just off the coast of the Clerke Peninsula. West of the Clerke Peninsula you can spend many hours exploring the reefs, islets and coves of the untouched Spanish Pilot Group. Or try fishing. "There's loads of snapper and salmon here and I never leave without one," boasted a local logger.

Portions of the coastline of Tlupana Inlet, north of Bligh Island, are lined with marble. Some of the smooth slabs that decorate the provincial legislature buildings in Victoria were quarried from this site seventy years ago.

Friendly Cove

Friendly Cove is a crossroads. Here the open ocean meets sheltered waterways. Here the Europeans made the first permanent contact with the native people of the coast. And here the British and Spanish empires intersected, with hostility and then peace.

The natives called Friendly Cove "Yuquot," after the Nootka tribe that inhabited it. Yuquot was one of the most important native fishing villages on the coast. A vast midden lies beneath the present-day buildings on the site. Today, the only permanent residents are a family who caretake the village for the Indian band. Upon arriving at Friendly Cove, report to the caretakers. Do not camp on Indian reserve land without permission.

A walk through the Indian reserve takes you past dilapidated structures, an ancient cemetery and along a trail paralleling the coastline to a freshwater lake. In centuries past, the Nootka whalers practiced their pre-hunt rites on the shores of the lake. Today, discarded shampoo bottles and soap containers are the discouraging reminders of contemporary bathers.

Church window, Friendly Cove

The steepled church, now rarely used, is a highlight at Friendly Cove. The stained-glass windows at the entrance of the church, donated by the Spanish government, illustrate the Spanish presence here almost two centuries ago.

A brightly-coloured lighthouse dominates Friendly Cove. The mighty beacon contrasts vividly with the lonely and exquisitely carved totem standing on the beach at Friendly Cove. They are fitting symbols of the two cultures that collided here. A short suspension bridge connects the lighthouse islet with Friendly Cove.

To mariners, especially those in small craft, a lighthouse is not merely a navigational aid. It is a bastion of humanity in the midst of an often hostile environment. Lighthouse keepers are an important part of the coast's outpost society. They do more than maintain the light. They monitor radio frequencies for distress calls, co-ordinate local rescue operations and record meteorological data. The lighthouse keepers at Friendly Cove have spent most of their working lives at various remote lighthouses on the coast. Their children have lived nowhere else, receiving an education through correspondence courses. One would certainly think twice before taking a long assignment in such an isolated place, but as one of the lighthouse keepers stated: "It's the cleanest air in Canada and you can't beat the view."

Cook Channel

Santa Gertrudis Cove is a well-protected and popular anchorage. It is possible to walk back to the lake behind the cove. Bocca del Infierno Bay — a lagoon — is accessible only at high slack. The neck of water at the entrance is a torrent at all other times. Climb up the bluffs above the rapids for a fine view of the serene lagoon and its frothy mouth. At Nootka village, only rusted boilers and a crumbling dock remain of the cannery that once operated here.

Near Boston Point, Chief Maquinna and the Nootkas revenged their mistreatment at the hands of the fur traders and massacred the crew of the fur trading ship *Boston* in 1803. Two men were taken as slaves. One of them, John R. Jewitt kept a journal, originally written in berry juice. It is one of the most important accounts of coastal native life. The traders were freed in 1805. Jewitt describes his parting with his captor, Chief Maquinna: "Grasping both my hands, with much emotion, while tears trickled down his cheeks, he bade me

177

farewell. I could not avoid experiencing a painful sensation on parting with the savage, who had preserved my life, and in general treated me with kindness and, considering their ideas and manner, much better than could have been expected."

Tahsis Inlet

Tahsis Inlet must be the most heavily logged waterway on the west coast of Canada. A large permanent logging camp is located at the north end of Kendrick Inlet. Local fishermen told us that the wind almost always blows north up the inlet. Thus, if you want to circumnavigate Nootka Island, it would be best to paddle north up the inlet and south on the outside, thereby maximizing the chance of tail winds. The jagged peaks overlooking the town of Tahsis will keep your eyes angled skyward as you proceed up the inlet. A pub-stop at the remote mill towns of Tahsis or Zeballos, which are a little off-route, makes an interesting change of pace. The tidal currents at both Tsowwin and Tahsis Narrows are not strong; you can paddle against them.

Esperanza Inlet

Esperanza Inlet is a museum of old villages, most of which are deserted. Ceepeecee, its name taken from the initials of the Canadian Packing Corporation, was once a regular stop on a steamship route. Its hospital, so tiny it was called the "Doll's House," once served 1500 people in the surrounding area. Only a few families inhabit Ceepeecee today. Across the water, the abandoned village of Hecate once had a pilchard reduction plant and a school. In 1925, the sardine-like pilchards suddenly populated the waters along the west coast of Vancouver Island in great numbers. The fish brought a new industry to Esperanza Inlet and five pilchard reduction plants were constructed here. Just as suddenly as it arrived, the mysterious fish vanished in 1945. The little village of Esperanza is a gem. In contrast to the others, it is tidy and well-kept. A Christian mission operates here now. Be sure to stop at the five-stool coffee shop for fresh pie and ice cream.

There are three Indian villages further west on Esperanza Inlet. The abandoned settlement at Ehatisaht has a beautiful totem pole, erected in 1910. The village site is overgrown with alder but a careful search may reveal a tombstone, a fruit tree growing through the

Ehatisaht totem pole

Sea canoeists, Catala Island

remains of a dugout canoe and burial caves. Indians presently inhabit villages at Queen Cove and Nuchatlitz. The area around Nuchatlitz is interesting. An old woman there weaves weed baskets. Local residents may allow visitors to inspect the burial caves nearby. Look for the remains of a shipwreck on the island northwest of Ensanada Islet. In the summer, drinking water is scarce at Nuchatlitz, so do not expect the villagers to share it.

Catala Island, near the mouth of Esperanza Inlet, has a fine sandy spit that juts into a body of water that a poet must have named: Rolling Roadstead. You may meet other paddlers in this area. A commercial outfit, based in Portland, Oregon, operates sea canoe expeditions here.

The Outer Coast

Between the exquisite sand beaches of Escalante and Burdwood on the south side of Nootka Sound and the reefs at the mouth of Esperanza Inlet, is thirty miles of wild, exposed coast. Due to the reefs, the shore's underwater shelf and frequent fog, only advanced paddlers should attempt this coastline. To find possible campsites, you must paddle close to shore, close to the reefs and surf. The swell can break irregularly over submerged rocks, causing unexpected eruptions. It is especially unnerving to be here in dense fog. The only thing good about the fog is that it masks the utter devastation of much of the forest here. Along this coast logging often begins right at the beach and ends way up a mountainside.

On Northwest Cone on Nootka Island, look for a World War II radar tower. A shipwreck is visible south of Ferrer Point. The Nootkas cut a trail from Ferrer Point all the way to Friendly Cove, and adventurous hikers still walk it. A trail also leads up Calvin Creek to Crawfish Lake. Bajo Point, Beano Creek and Maquinna Point were ancient Indian fishing sites. Extensive kelp beds border much of the shoreline. Scallop and abalone are plentiful on this wild coast.

VANCOUVER ISLAND

BROOKS BAY

Brooks Peninsula

Cape Cook

JOHNSON LAGOON

NASPART INLET

Jackobson Point

Acous Peninsula

O'LEARY ITS.: CHECKAKLIS IS.:

CHECKLESET BAY

Clerke Point

'CLARA IT.

BATTLE BAY

OUOUKINSH INLET

BUNSBY ISLANDS

HOLLYWOOD

KASHUTL INLET

TAHSISH RIVER

TAHSISH INLET

Markale Peninsula FAIR HARBOUR

AMAI INLET

CACHALOT INLET

CACHALOT CR.

CACHALOT CR.

ESPERANZA INLET

THOMAS IS.

CLANNINICK COVE

McLEAN ISLAND

CHAMISS BAY

BRITISH CR.

KYUQUOT

UNION ISLAND

Rugged Point

GROGAN ROCK

GRASSY IS.

BARRIER ISLANDS

Tatchu Point

PACIFIC OCEAN

KYUQUOT SOUND

N

KYUQUOT AREA

0   2   4   6   8 n.m.

Kyuquot Area

Area 17

Attractions: Indian culture, past and present. Large sea bird colonies. Abundant wildlife: sea lion, sea otter, wolf, bear. The remote, otherworldly east coast of the Brooks Peninsula. Challenging exposed coast paddling.

Access: From the town of Campbell River on Vancouver Island, drive north on Highway 19 for approximately 155 km. Watch for signs indicating the logging road turnoff to Zeballos. The use of the road is sometimes restricted due to logging activity. Follow the logging road past Zeballos to Fair Harbour and launch there. Allow four hours for the drive from Campbell River to Fair Harbour.

Seascape: Inside Kyuquot Sound the waterways are sheltered. The outer coast is exposed to the ocean winds and swell, but only the stretch between Kyuquot village and the Bunsby Islands lacks protective cover.

Hazards: Heavy seas along the exposed coast. Frequent fog. Between the village of Kyuquot and Esperanza Inlet: a chain of reefs and islets, many of which lie just below the water level at high tide.

Season: April to October. Driest in July and August. Never crowded.

Length: 5 to 14 days.

Camping: Many sand or pebble beaches. Bears and wolves are common. Stash food away from camp.

Charts: 3682 Kyuquot Sound   1:36,700
             3683 Checleset Bay   1:36,500

Introduction

There are many highlights on this trip: an ancient Indian fortress, totem poles camouflaged by the forest, the rare sea otter, a remote fishing village, beaches that have known few footprints. Many who paddle here stay within the protected waters of Kyuquot Sound and poke into the ocean only for day trips, yet the voyage up to the Brooks Peninsula requires only moderate sea kayaking experience. If the ocean gets too rough, you can hide behind the islands and peninsulas along the rugged coastline. The 5½ miles between Kyuquot village and the Bunsby Islands is the only stretch lacking any shelter.

The logging road leading from Highway 19 to Zeballos and Fair Harbour is often in rough condition, but is passable in normal passenger cars. There are just a few shacks at Fair Harbour. Curiously, this seaside village was abandoned as soon as the road connected it with civilization. At Zeballos you will find stores, a gas station and a pub.

Fair Harbour to Union Island

Fill up the water containers at the pipe at Fair Harbour before departing. Paddling out of Fair Harbour, underneath the mountains called "Family Humps," you can avoid the extra distance around the Markale Peninsula by portaging at the 100-metre wide Markale isthmus. A detour up the Tahsish Inlet (not to be confused with the Tahsis Inlet further south on Vancouver Island) will take you to the Tahsish River. The virgin watershed and estuary here contrast vividly with the logging-scarred slopes en route. The Tahsish River has an exceptional salmon run, has a good steelhead population, and is a winter habitat for elk. The area may be logged. The Kyuquot-Tahsish Committee, a conservation group, is trying to save this fine watershed.

For eons man has harvested the timber in Kyuquot Sound. The Kyuquot Indians were the first loggers. In the woods adjacent to Kashutl Inlet modern lumbermen found an almost fully carved dugout canoe. A fault deep within the timber had ruined the carver's labour.

A large logging camp has operated for decades at Chamiss Bay, north of Union Island. Before the advent of logging trucks, timber was hauled out of the bush by rail. Tracks are still visible at British Creek, just south of Chamiss Bay. On the other side of Union Island, the ruins at Cachalot Creek, at the mouth of Cachalot Inlet, are all that remain of a whaling station.

Handlogging, a dying art, is still practiced in Kyuquot Sound. Handloggers are multi-talented individuals who selectively log shoreline timbers, using only a chain saw, cable and tugboat. Considerable skill is required to fall a tree such that it can be hauled out of the bush and into the sea by the tug. It is interesting to watch handloggers at work, but you should do this only from a distance.

Rugged Point to Esperanza Inlet

One of the finest beaches on Vancouver Island faces the ocean at Rugged Point. If you do not want to surf onto the exposed beach, land at the sheltered beach behind the point, just within the mouth of Kyuquot Sound. In rough weather, paddlers have sheltered at the cabin here. A trail leads across to the exposed beach. You might share a campfire with loggers who occasionally hike in from camps along Esperanza Inlet, especially on summer weekends.

The wave-lashed rocks and islets south of Rugged Point deserve cautious exploration. They are home for thousands of birds, including storm petrels, gulls, pigeon guillemots and tufted puffins. Grogan Rock is a distinctive offshore pinnacle. The soft hues of Grassy Island almost glow against the blank ocean horizon. Landing on one of the islets here, we discovered many rocks stamped with the design of a shell; the islet is a mound of fossil. A nearby reef, strewn with lumber, seems to have grabbed at a passing ship. Ironically, amongst the wreckage we found a Japanese glass float the size of a soccer ball, cradled by a rocky crag.

Kyuquot Village

The isolated settlement of Kyuquot is a droplet of civilization in the sea. There is a store, a school, even a little hospital which flies the flag of the Red Cross. The colourful houses here have a cheerful aspect. Float planes buck the ocean winds to land in the harbour.

People are the main attraction of Kyuquot. Every time we visited this remote outpost we met a person with an interesting story. A trawler skipper told us that earlier in the day he had spotted a group of elephant seals, a few miles offshore. Distinguished by a long tubular snout, these monsters are the largest seals in the world. The fisherman advised that the best time to observe another undersea giant, the grey whale, is during their annual migration along this coast in late March and late September.

Kyuquot is one of the most important supply stops for the pleasure boaters that cruise the west coast of Vancouver Island. The yachtsmen who navigate this coast are usually of the adventurous type, and we heard more than one account of a trans-oceanic voyage. These people were often surprised to learn that a kayak was also a long-distance cruising vessel, and could see its advantages in exploring reef-strewn, surf-bashed areas like the exposed coast near Kyuquot.

At the government dock we talked with one of the old men of the Indian village who had come down to look at our boats. When asked for the time, he replied "Slow time or fast time?" He did not believe in Daylight Saving Time. He poined out "Miss Charlie," a seal, nosing about our kayaks. An orphan, she had grown up in the harbour as the community's pet.

The last tribal battle on the coast was fought in 1855 between the Kyuquots and the Clayoquots on the islands directly south of the village. In one night of war almost one hundred people were killed.

Bunsby Islands

West of Kyuquot, look for large sea caves along the shores of Gregory and McLean Islands, and listen for the blowhole tom-toms. Paddling the stream at Clanninick Cove, you are swallowed by the forest. An ecological reserve protects the alluvial Sitka spruces here.

Bunsby Islands

The open passage up to Bunsby Islands is best paddled in the morning while the sea is generally calm. A natural tunnel bores through Thomas Island, the mid-point on the route. Over a thousand storm petrels nest on the island. The Bunsby Islands, named after a character in a Dickens novel, should not be missed. Their soft beauty pleases all visitors. The Checleset Indian band once populated these islands and recently a few have returned to the Indian reserve, known locally as "Hollywood," on the mainland adjacent to the Bunsbys. The Checlesets of another age chose a dramatic location for their fortress. Situated on Checkaklis Island and surrounded by terraces of fruit trees and flowers, it overlooks a distinctive rock which towers out of the ocean depths.

The early fur traders wiped out the west coast's sea otter population. Checleset Bay is the site of an international project to bring these furry creatures back, and the bay is now protected as an ecological reserve. Between 1969 and 1972, the animals were transported here from the Gulf of Alaska. They seem to have taken to their new habitat. We spotted a number of them. They have unusual eating habits. Floating face up, they prepare meals of sea urchins or crabs on their bellies, using stones to crack the shells. Watch the sea otter show business at the "Hollywood" Indian reserve.

Acous Peninsula

From Ououkinsh Inlet all the way around the Brooks Peninsula and up to Klaskino Inlet, the mountain slopes of the coastline are untouched. Paddling north from the Bunsbys, we discovered the abandoned native village on the Acous Peninsula. Here again, the natives chose a special place: a semi-circular pebble beach, protected from the heaving ocean by the lonely tree-whisped islets offshore. The Indians buried their dead on one of the islets, and a crumbling dugout canoe there still contains skeletal remains. Two totem poles project out of the salal bushes behind the cove. One is weathered, smooth and featureless. An expert craftsman must have carved the

Acous totem pole

188

other. In the bush you will find a toppled truss and post of an Indian longhouse.

The Indians held potlatches on the banks of the river east of Acous, in Battle Bay. What a place! The river curves around the sand bank and then pushes a channel through the surf, making a perfect landing spot. Trout wiggle through the water upstream. Here we witnessed a deer avoid the chops of a pursuing wolf by dashing along the river bank into the sea. Paddle upriver and take a refreshing bath in one of the pools.

Smell, look and listen for sea lion rookeries on the islets a couple of miles out in the ocean, south of Acous Peninsula. The O'Leary Islets have a large herd and it sometimes visits the Clara Islets. Excluded bulls smother rocky outcroppings away from the main colony.

Brooks Peninsula

Jutting ten miles out into the Pacific, the angular skyline of the Brooks has the profile of a key. The eastern shore of this untouched hinterland is magical. (The next section of this chapter discusses the rest of the Brooks Peninsula.) It is not possible to be further from civilization on Vancouver Island. In the lee of the prevailing northwest winds in the summer, this coast of the Brooks is lashed at other times of the year by southeast storms which blow the driftwood right into the forests. Due to the severity of the environment, few people have lived on the Brooks. The Indians once had a fishing camp near Clerke Point but only a shelter stands there now. There is an intermittently occupied squatter's shack behind Jackobson Point. Three of its occupants mysteriously disappeared a few years ago while paddling in Checleset Bay.

A trip up Nasparti Inlet is worthwhile if only to see the reversing tidal falls at the mouth of Johnson Lagoon. You can paddle in and out of the lagoon only at high tide. The creeks which flow into Nasparti Inlet are congested with ducks and geese. You might even spot a trumpeter swan.

From Jackobson Point to Clerke Point the coastline is incessantly frothy. A deep creek cleaves the beautiful sand beach next to Jackobson Point. A perfect spot for a sauna. For those who do not want to tackle the surf, a trail leads from the protected shores behind Jackobson Point to the beach. You can spend days hiking this exceptional coastline.

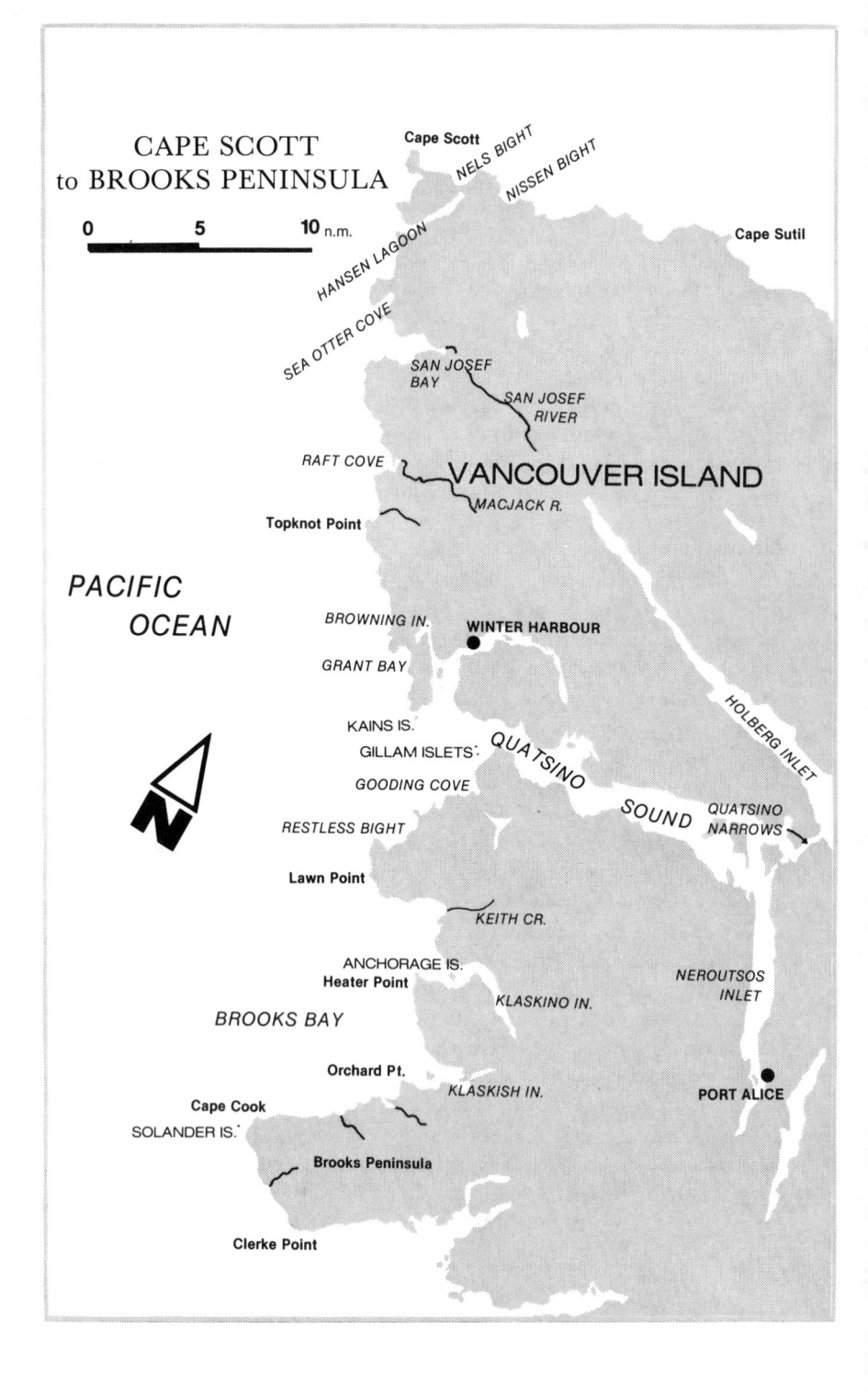

CAPE SCOTT
to BROOKS PENINSULA

0   5   10 n.m.

Cape Scott
NELS BIGHT
NISSEN BIGHT
Cape Sutil

HANSEN LAGOON

SEA OTTER COVE

SAN JOSEF BAY
SAN JOSEF RIVER

RAFT COVE

VANCOUVER ISLAND

MACJACK R.

Topknot Point

PACIFIC OCEAN

BROWNING IN.   WINTER HARBOUR

GRANT BAY

KAINS IS.
GILLAM ISLETS
GOODING COVE

QUATSINO SOUND

HOLBERG INLET

QUATSINO NARROWS

RESTLESS BIGHT

Lawn Point

KEITH CR.

ANCHORAGE IS.
Heater Point

NEROUTSOS INLET

KLASKINO IN.

BROOKS BAY

Orchard Pt.

KLASKISH IN.

PORT ALICE

Cape Cook
SOLANDER IS.

Brooks Peninsula

Clerke Point

Cape Scott to Brooks Peninsula

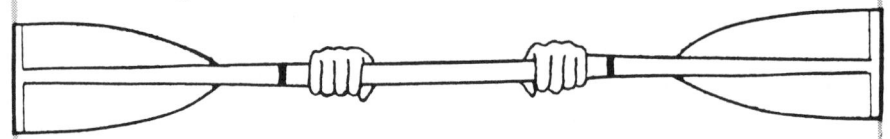

Area 18

Attractions: The most exciting stretch of coastline on Vancouver Island, a challenge even to the most advanced sea kayaker. The Brooks Peninsula: an ecological treasure.

Access: Drive or fly to the town of Port Hardy at the northern end of Highway 19 on Vancouver Island. Drive 42 km east on the unpaved road to the town of Holberg. At Holberg, signs indicate the 16 km long logging road to Cape Scott Provincial Park. Launch at the San Josef River near the boundary of the park. Alternatively, from Holberg follow the signs indicating Winter Harbour, a 14 km drive south along logging roads. Launch at the public wharf there. Bus service to and from Winter Harbour connects with some of the Pacific Western jet flights at Port Hardy. Restrictions on the use of the logging road are posted on road signs.

Seascape: Open ocean. Heavy swell. Frequent gales.

Hazards: The entire coastline can be a hazard to inexperienced ocean paddlers. Tidal currents make the waters off Cape Scott particularly treacherous. Expect high winds near Cape Cook.

Season: June to September. Storms least likely in August.

Length: 3 to 14 days. Allow 3 days minimum if the trip is confined to the Cape Scott area. For the trip from Winter Harbour to the Brooks Peninsula and back allow at least a week.

Camping: Deserted sand beaches, many accessible only through surf. Protect food from bear and wolf.

Charts: 3617 Quatsino Sound   1:48,700
       3624 Cape Cook to Cape Scott   1:90,000
       3680 Brooks Bay   1:38,300

West Coast - Vancouver Island

Introduction

One word describes the sea kayaking experience between Cape Scott and the Brooks Peninsula: wild. Along with the west side of the Queen Charlotte Islands, this area offers the most challenging paddling on Canada's west coast. Only advanced sea kayakers should venture here.

The sea kayak is the best vessel in which to explore this unprotected stretch of coastline. It can thread the reefs, ride the swell and punch through the surf. The deserted lengths of golden sand are a beachcomber's paradise with glass floats, fishing lures, whale bones, the tracks of wolf, cougar and bear. A paddler we met found a waterproofed box of Japanese candy. The thick forest behind the beaches is virtually untouched. This unfriendly environment has prevented man from intruding far. Yet the thundering seas, the gales and the desolation are precisely why competent kayakers visit here. It is not possible to be closer to the great powers of nature.

Winds are lightest in the morning here, and this is the best time for travel. Even in the early hours you must be wary of the thermal winds which blow out of the river valleys and inlets. By noon the westerlies or northwesterlies can reach 25 knots or more, subsiding only in the evening.

Of the two launching spots, Winter Harbour, near the mouth of Quatsino Sound, is the most centrally located and protected. Starting at the San Josef River further north, you may have to paddle through surf at San Josef Bay. If you are planning a one-way, long-distance trip south along the west coast of Vancouver Island, start at the San Josef River — it is the most northerly road-end launching spot. If you are flying in, the pilot will probably land at Sea Otter Cove. A float plane can get in and out of Hansen Lagoon, near Cape Scott, only at high tide.

Cape Scott Provincial Park

The park preserves almost 15,000 wilderness hectares of the northwest tip of Vancouver Island, from San Josef Bay in the south to Nissen Bight in the north. Trails lead from the parking area at the end of the logging road to both the west and north coasts of the park. Along the north coast, a trail leads past Hansen Lagoon and Nels Bight to the Cape Scott lighthouse. In the summer it is not uncommon to see hikers trekking the many kilometres of surf-battered beaches along the park's coastline. The beach at the mouth of the San Josef River, a two-hour hike from the parking lot, is the most popular. Kayakers must have previous surf experience before landing at such beaches. The San Josef River cuts a channel through its sand delta, breaking the surf except in high seas. Fishboats frequently hide in the partially sheltered waters of San Josef Bay and Sea Otter Cove.

The Cape Scott area was the site of a heroic attempt to settle and farm this inhospitable territory in 1897, and again in 1910. The elements defeated the Danish pioneers. A few weathered buildings and the names on the chart are all they left behind. (See *The Cape Scott Story* by Lester Peterson.) Hansen Lagoon is a vast mud flat, except at high tide. Prime waterfowl habitat, it vibrates with the honks and flaps of thousands of ducks and geese. It is an important stopover for birds migrating along the Pacific flyway. If you want to explore the lagoon by kayak, follow the narrow channel which parallels the western shore. At the end of the lagoon you will find a large meadow behind ancient dykes. A short hike from the lagoon will take you to Nels Bight, a magnificent expanse of white sand.

The great tidal currents that flow around Cape Scott make the waters here particularly unstable, at times forcing even big seine fishing boats to retreat. Paddling around Cape Scott is only sensible in calm weather. It is a short portage across the narrow, sandy isthmus that connects Cape Scott with Vancouver Island, but due to the surf which can pound either side of the isthmus, this shortcut might be more troublesome than travelling around the cape. On the south side of the isthmus are the ruins of a World War II RCAF camp.

San Josef Bay to Quatsino Sound

Paddling the deep swell on this coastline is like riding a roller coaster, and you may feel seasick until your body adjusts to the topsy-turvy motion. The first major beach south of San Josef Bay is at Raft Cove. The sand flats are so expansive than an airplane in distress once successfully landed here. A rocky outcropping near the north end of the beach permits a surfless landing. Imprints of bear and wolf form trails in the sand, but human tracks are rare. A well-kept trapper's cabin is nestled in the underbrush on the south side of the Macjack River. Though the river is deep and has a wide mouth, it fails to break the surf. Two miles south is another fine beach and river

Capsize!

estuary near Topknot Point.

Grant Bay is the next significant stretch of sand. A frail prospector's cabin protrudes from the thimbleberry and salal bushes behind the beach. Do not rely on the charted creek at Grant Bay for water. In dry weather nothing trickles out of its log-jammed estuary. The fishboats which frequently anchor in the bay may be able to supply some fresh water. Mid-point on the beach, a trail leads back to the marshes of Browning Lagoon.

In the summer the horseflies along this stretch of coastline can be vicious.

Quatsino Sound

With a military base, open-pit mine, pulp mill and logging scars, the inner lengths of Quatsino Sound are too trampled by man to be of interest to most kayakers, except perhaps for weekend trips.

The village of Winter Harbour near the mouth of the sound serves a large fishing fleet and has a laundry, shower, public telephone, cafe, post office and well-stocked store. The fishboats with the chimney-blackened stabilizing sails are deep-sea tuna boats.

The residents of the small villages which dot Canada's west coast are usually the best source of practical information about the adjacent sea kayaking area. We spent an hour in the coffee shop at Winter Harbour and left with our chart covered with notes. One of the local fishermen recommended the salmon fishing near the Kains Island lighthouse at the northern entrance to Quatsino Sound. We followed his advice and a four-minute troll earned a six-pound coho.

The Gillam Islets at the mouth of Quatsino Sound have a large sea bird colony: over 3,000 storm petrels nest here. You will hear eerie noises in this vicinity. They emanate from a floating fog whistle.

It is thrilling to thread your kayak through the archipelago of rocks strewn between Gooding Cove and Restless Bight. The ocean waves thunder over the offshore pinnacles, creating a score of miniature waterfalls. Paddlers can land at the sheltered bays north of Restless Bight or behind a protrusion at the extreme north end of the bight.

Lawn Point is a delightful geographic anomaly. This flat, treeless snout poking into the surf looks completely out of place, surrounded by rain-forested mountain slopes. If the grass were not shoulder-high you could play football here. In the middle of the "lawn" stands a slim weather tower: a white man's totem pole. The seas are particularly wild here, but it is easy to land behind the point. A World War II plane crashed in the bush nearby. Only one person walked away from the wreck, and he has never been found.

Brooks Bay

Lashed by almost perpetual ocean-born wind and wave, these waters can quicken the pulse of even a jaded seafarer. Fortunately, Klaskino and Klaskish Inlets provide cover when the going gets too rough. The beaches lining Brooks Bay have an unusual bounty: Japanese glass balls. We met three kayakers here who had collected over a hundred such prizes in ten days. The stream that empties onto the pebble beach across from Anchorage Island in Klaskino Inlet (not the Indian reserve beach), has an enchanting waterfall and deep pools. It could be Eden.

In the many sandy estuaries that interrupt the Brooks Bay

The Brooks from the air

Estuary at Brooks Bay

shoreline you will find tasty nourishment: crabs. Drop a crab trap and a few hours later you will pull up dinner.

Ten miles long and six miles wide and protruding further into the Pacific Ocean than any other headland on Canada's west coast, the Brooks Peninsula seems to have every environmental nuance that the west coast can offer: stilletto peaks, alpine lakes and meadows, a broad, lush river estuary, and a long, varied shoreline of sand and stone; all undisturbed by man. Scientific evidence suggests that the Brooks Peninsula was one of the few areas on the coast to escape glaciation in the last ice age. You need no scientific training to appreciate that the Brooks is indeed special. Sadly, the provincial Mines Ministry vetoed a proposal that a portion of the Brooks be protected as an ecological reserve.

To land your kayak on the Brooks Peninsula anywhere between the entrance of Klaskish Inlet and Cape Cook, it is almost impossible to avoid surf, big surf. The two major river estuaries on this side of the Brooks, very rarely visited by man, speak of another world, another epoch and are worth a wrestle through the waves.

Cape Cook to Clerke Point

There are many natural delights near Cape Cook, but this is no place to explore except on a rare calm day. In the two bays immediately northeast of the cape, look for a big sea cave and paddle right into the home base of a fleet of seals. Nearby is a fine waterfall and pool. Follow the river upstream to alpine meadows. The vegetation near Cape Cook reflects the severity of the environment. The forest ends just a few hundred metres above the sea. Only scrubby dwarf pines can survive the storms and sea spray. The area resembles a vast bog.

Solander Island is an ecological reserve. A large colony of tufted puffins, over 3,000 pairs, cling to its rocky ledges. Storm petrels and Cassin's auklets also nest here. Sea lions inhabit the offshore rocks. It is possible to land on this treeless, windswept island, but only in calm weather. If you have packed a telephoto lens you will be rewarded here. The tufted puffins with their distinctive beaks and prismatic wardrobes are extremely photogenic.

We rounded Cape Cook in the early morning but even then the winds were howling. We encountered the largest forest of kelp here that we have ever seen. It seemed to cover square miles of the sea. The mat of kelp flattened the swell, and we glided over it propelled just by the gale. It is essential to have a knife handy here. The nose of our boat submarined under kelp stalks and we were almost sommersaulted by a wave. It is virtually impossible to lift the leafy kelp off the boat, but the knife glides easily through even a wrist-thick stalk. We encountered no surf on the stream-washed beach mid-point on the southwest coast of the Brooks. The shelter at the Indian reserve near Clerke Point might be useful in a storm.

Chapter Nine
THE QUEEN CHARLOTTE ISLANDS

And finally, the Queen Charlotte Islands: Canada's west coast quintessence. Befitting its position as an extremity — extending further into the Pacific Ocean than any other part of Canada — the environment and people of this wedge-shaped archipelago are expressions of intensity. The islands sit in the most active earthquake zone in the country. The ocean expends more energy thundering ashore here than any other coastline of equivalent length in Canada. Few other places in the Pacific Ocean are given more respect by skippers than Hecate Strait, which separates the Queen Charlottes from the mainland.

In spite of the severity of the environment, life on the islands is staggeringly exuberant. The stands of spruce, hemlock and red cedar are amongst the largest on the planet. Some of the richest shellfish beds on the entire Pacific coast are found here. Well over one quarter of all the sea birds on Canada's west coast nest in these islands. Botanists have found flora here that grow nowhere else.

The people of the islands mirror their extraordinary environment. At its zenith, the Haida Indian culture was one of the richest of any pre-industrial peoples. Ferocity, practicality and artistry blended to form the unique Haida character. Warriors paddled 800 kilometres in dugout canoes to plunder rival tribes. The Queen Charlotte natives were so effective in exploiting the wealth of the sea and forest that they could support an entire subculture of carvers, whose craftmanship is the Haida's greatest legacy. Modern sea kayakers are among the beneficiaries of some of this art. On the paddling route is the totem forest at the abandoned village of Ninstints, recently designated by UNESCO as an International Heritage Site. The Queen Charlottes' shoreline reveals the colourful thread of white man's history as well: an ancient mining shaft, a mountainside boardwalk, a whaling station, even the remains of an oil rig from the turn of the century.

For a superb history of the Queen Charlottes, see *The Queen Charlotte Islands Book 2 of Places and Names* by Kathleen A. Dalzell. This volume is especially useful to kayakers as it discusses the history of the islands on a place-by-place basis. See also *Klee Wyck* by Emily Carr in which the famous painter describes her experiences at the many now-abandoned Indian villages on the paddling routes discussed in this chapter. A useful visitors guide to the Charlottes is *A Guide to the Queen Charlotte Islands* by Neil G. Carey.

The people who inhabit the Queen Charlottes today continue the uncommon lifestyle of their predecessors. One has to be a character to live on these wild, remote islands. And that is the magic of the Queen Charlotte Islands. Nothing here is mediocre.

If your boat can be transported by aircraft, getting to the Queen Charlottes is easy. Daily Pacific Western jet flights connect Sandspit and Vancouver. Trans-Provincial Airlines operates float plane service between Prince Rupert and Sandspit. British Columbia Ferries cross Hecate Strait from Prince Rupert to Skidegate (near Queen Charlotte City), three times weekly in the summer. The trip takes approximately eight hours. From Vancouver, Prince Rupert is two days' travel by land or sea. The 1503 kilometre highway drive through British Columbia's interior is one route option, but an alternative is to drive to Port Hardy on Vancouver Island and take the ferry along the inside passage to Prince Rupert. Car reservations for such a trip must be made months in advance.

Queen Charlotte City on Graham Island is the administrative hub of the Queen Charlottes, and it has all the services a kayaker needs. "Charlotte," as the residents call it, has approximately 1,000 inhabitants, many of whom are young people. Skidegate is the native village, five kilometres east of Queen Charlotte City. A fine museum displaying Haida artifacts and totem poles is located at Second Beach, near the village. Paddlers wishing to visit the abandoned Haida village sites discussed in this chapter *must* apply for permission at the band council office in Skidegate. The application

The Haida legacy

must be made during office hours. Authorization can sometimes be arranged by mail. A short ferry-ride across Skidegate Inlet to Alliford Bay and an eleven-kilometre drive will take you to Sandspit. The jets from Vancouver land at the Sandspit airport. You will also find a fine pub and hotel here. Birdwatching is excellent along the spit.

The two trips discussed in the following pages cover the 120 miles between Sandspit and Anthony Island. The richness of the sea kayaking experience here cannot be overstated. One major attribute of this coastline is that it lies within a rain shadow. Although the high rainfall on some parts of the Queen Charlottes is legendary, the east coast of Moresby Island, between May and August, receives almost exactly the same amount of rain as Sechelt's "Sunshine Coast" — one of the coast's driest spots. July and August are easily the best months to visit because of their accommodating temperatures.

The Queen Charlotte Islands present many other touring possibilities. Three deserve mention here. The lazy paddler will enjoy canal-like Masset Sound on Graham Island. Its strong tidal current (which can reach nine knots) sweeps the paddler through twenty miles of lowland territory, past old homesteads and logging settlements.

Kayak adventurers may consider touring the west side of the Queen Charlotte Islands. A voyage down Skidegate Inlet, out to the unsheltered northwest coast of Moresby Island, and then back into one of the protected inlets (such as Peel Inlet which is accessible by logging road) will expose you to the wild side of the Queen Charlottes. You will pass the abandoned Haida villages of Chaatl and Kaisun on this route. An even more challenging trip is along the west coast of Graham Island. Between Hippa Island and Tian Head there is much to explore: rocky headlands, overgrown Indian villages, shipwrecks, abandoned cabins, pristine streams and lakes. Although there are many sheltered inlets, most of this coast is battered by the sea. Only advanced sea paddlers should venture here. Float planes are the only means of transport to and from this area.

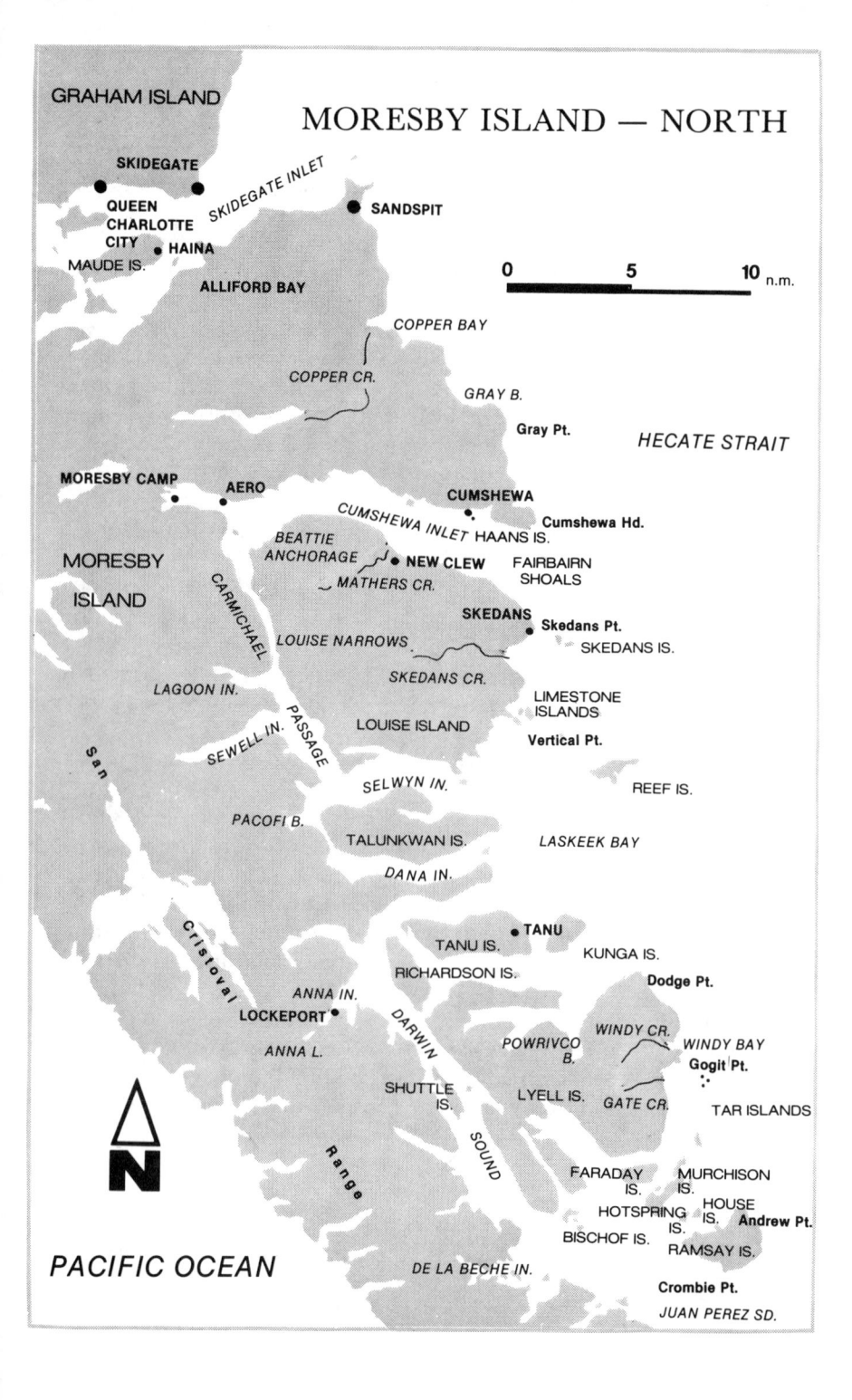

Moresby Island — North

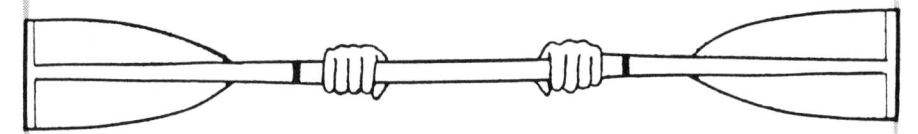

Area 19

Attractions: Abandoned settlements: totem poles and logging relics. A smorgasbord from the sea. Sea bird and sea lion colonies. Mountain scenery. An island of hot springs.

Access: Fly to Sandspit from either Vancouver or Prince Rupert, or take the ferry from Prince Rupert to Skidegate. At Sandspit, launch in the waters directly adjacent to the airport or drive south via logging roads and launch at Moresby Camp or Gray Bay. At Skidegate, launch in the water near the ferry landing, or take the car ferry across to Moresby Island and launch at either Sandspit, Moresby Camp or Gray Bay.

Seascape: Exposed only to the east. Little swell. Cover provided by offshore islands. Suitable for all kayakers except beginners.

Hazards: Disturbed seas are common at several locations including: the shoals near Sandspit, the Fairbairn Shoals at the mouth of Cumshewa Inlet, Skedans Point on Louise Island and Gogit Point and Dodge Point on Lyell Island.

Season: May to September. Mildest in July and August.

Length: 7 to 14 days.

Camping: The area is blessed with camping sites. Permission from the Indian band in Skidegate is required to visit the following Indian reserves: Haina, New Clew, Cumshewa, Skedans and Tanu. Camping is not allowed at these sites.

Charts:		
3897 Atli Inlet to Selwyn Inlet	1:37,500
3808 Juan Perez Sound	1:37,500
3853 Cape St. James to Cumshewa Inlet	1:150,000
3894 Selwyn Inlet to Lawn Point	1:73,000

Introduction

Few areas in the world offer the sea kayaker as many delights as the coastline between Queen Charlotte City and Hotspring Island. At the end of a paddling trip here, you will have acquired a treasure of experience. There is so much to enjoy. The deserted native villages seem haunted, as if their former residents were still walking about the totem poles and longhouses. The abandoned settlements of the white man are almost as intriguing. These outposts are now industrial graveyards, where the curious will find the skeletons of the white man's machines. The natural history of this area is just as rewarding as the history of man. The wilderness is spectacularly rich. For the paddling naturalist, photographer, seafood connoisseur or diver, the northeast coast of Moresby Island guarantees a satisfying trip.

It is not essential to have a motor vehicle on the Queen Charlotte Islands to get to the recommended launching spots. You can start your paddle in the waters near where you exit either the plane or ferry which brought you to the Charlottes. If you want to avoid the developed coastline between Queen Charlotte City and Gray Bay, you must launch at Moresby Camp or Gray Bay and this requires a vehicle. You can rent a van from one of the rental agencies in Sandspit or Queen Charlotte City, or hire a taxi. The route from Sandspit south to both Moresby Camp and Gray Bay follows active logging roads and public use is generally restricted to evenings and Sundays. For details, inquire at the forestry company offices (Crown Zellerbach and MacMillan Bloedel) in Sandspit. The route to Moresby Camp lacks direction signs and even local drivers get lost in the labyrinth of logging roads.

For the journey south to Hotspring Island and back, paddle the east side of Louise and Lyell Island in one direction and the inside route in the other direction. A one-way trip is also possible. From Queen Charlotte City you may be able to hitch a ride south on one of the fishing or pleasure boats which you will find at the government docks. You may have to wait a few days before you find a generous skipper going in your direction. The alternative is to hire a ride down to Hotspring Island. Be prepared to pay between $250.00 and $500.00 for such transportation. You may have better luck hitching a ride from Hotspring Island back to Queen Charlotte City than the reverse. For those with collapsible boats, Trans-Provincial Airlines will charter both Beaver and Single Otter aircraft from Sandspit to

Murchison Island (next to Hotspring Island). As the wind blows mainly from the north or northwest in the summer months, a one-way trip south, rather than north, is recommended.

Queen Charlotte City to Cumshewa Head

The surface of Skidegate Inlet is rarely flat. The wind and innumerable boat wakes toss the water. Opposite Queen Charlotte City is the site of the Haina village on Maude Island. Like other Haida villages, it was abandoned around the turn of the century when the Haida who survived white man's diseases regrouped in Skidegate and Masset. At Haina, you will find an overgrown orchard. Further south, at Alliford Bay on Moresby Island, the RCAF operated a seaplane base for the flying boats that patrolled the coast in World War II. Only the concrete survived the ending of the war.

From Alliford Bay all the way around to Cumshewa Head, the shoreline is a bracelet of sand and pebble, studded with boulders. Treat the tidal currents flowing over the Sandspit shoals with respect.

Over a century ago, miners sunk a deep shaft (now filled) at Copper Bay. Copper Creek and Bay are popular with sports fishermen. At the southern tip of the seemingly endless beach at Gray Bay is a now defunct loran station. The road from Sandspit ends here. Find sand beaches indent the coastline between Gray Bay and Cumshewa Head.

Carmichael Passage to Dana Inlet

If you launch at Moresby Camp, the most interesting route south is along Cumshewa Inlet and around Skedans Point. An alternative, perhaps on the return journey, is the inside route between Louise Island and Moresby Island. The width of Carmichael Passage is pinched to a few boat lengths at Louise Narrows. This is best traversed at slack, or when the tide is flowing in your direction.

Since the turn of the century white man has been active along this stretch of the Moresby coast. Lagoon Inlet (tidal rapids block the lagoon entrance, except at slack tide) had a cannery and logging camp. The logging camp at Sewell Inlet is still active today. At Pacofi Bay, an unusual cement structure, still visible, spawned rumours that the German-built fish plant was a front for a pre-World War II U-boat base. The name of the bay derives from the Pacific Coast Fishery

Company, which operated a fish reduction plant.

Cumshewa Inlet

As the tidal current is significant here, try to leave Moresby Camp on an ebb tide. Teredo-chewed piles mark the old logging camp at Aero. Timber-tugging locomotives once puffed through the woods here. Deer, bear, racoon and mink roam the shoreline. Mt. Moresby, spotted with snow even in the summer, stabs at the sky at the head of Cumshewa Inlet.

The abandoned Haida village of Cumshewa is typical of the dozens of native sites along the coast of the Queen Charlotte Islands. All that remain are a midden, a grassy open space and crumbling totem poles. In addition, tomb-like mounds, apparently mass graves of smallpox victims from the 1870's, bulge the ground under weathered fruit trees. At low water, a causeway joins the village with Haans Island.

Much of the north coast of Louise Island has been picked clean by the loggers from the Beattie Anchorage logging camp at the mouth of Carmichael Passage. Trucks, stacked high with timber and noisy as dive bombers, swoop down from the mountains and along the north

Logging relics, Mathers Creek

coast road to the camp. At Mathers Creek; the logging days of old come alive again. In the forest just east of the creek, look for the double-tracked wooden logging road and the rusted fleet of trucks that rolled along it. You will find a few flattened cabins from the logging camp built on the site of the nearby Indian village of New Clew. A cannery here once rendered oil from the livers of dogfish. A few grave stones leaning at odd angles are sad testimony to the diseases which ravaged the village in the nineteenth century. A well-tended cabin, used by government fisheries personnel, is hidden in the woods near the mouth of the creek. Upriver you will find a fish hatchery.

A vast tangle of kelp blankets a large area of the east end of Cumshewa Inlet. Grab a stalk — a natural anchor — and examine the marine underworld here. Observe the kelp crab perform tightrope acrobatics along the kelp stalks.

Skedans

Except for the village of Ninstints on Anthony Island, the village of Skedans on the eastern point of Louise Island has the largest number of totems in their original location on Canada's west coast. Most of the monuments have fallen. One of the standing totems is notable for its fluted design, unique among Haida carvings. The Indians interred the corpses of important people in wooden boxes atop many of these poles.

Of the two back-to-back beaches at Skedans, the northern one is preferable for landing, as the other is choked with logs, stuffed into the bay by southeast storms. A cave at the waterline between the two beaches emits a hollow moan. Unfortunately, the noisy helicopters which invade the beach and disgorge tourists for fifteen minute snapshot sessions interfere with the special character of Skedans. So does the logging scar on the hill above the village. The logging on the Indian reserve was done in the mid 1960's — before the Indian band was as conservation-oriented as it is now.

Sea lions occupy the most exposed of the Skedans Islands. The massive animals will belly-flop into the sea at the approach of an intruder, so when there are a number of kayakers, paddle to the colony in a group to enable everyone to see the roaring beasts. A large population of fork-tailed storm petrels nest on the Skedans Islands. Look for giant mussels (the orange flesh is delicious) on the islands'

Skedans Islands

rocky outcroppings.

Vertical Point to Tanu

The narrow, flat isthmus in the middle of the peninsula at Vertical Point was once a Haida settlement. Nearby is a lonely, intermittently occupied cabin. A meadow of tall grass, foxglove, mint and a neglected garden separate the forest from the sea. The Limestone Islands, just north of Vertical Point, are home for a large colony of ancient murrelets. If the water is calm, paddle out to the sea lion rocks off the eastern tip of Reef Island. The Haida once had a fort on this inhospitable island. Watch for peregrine falcons speeding through the sky along the coast of Reef Island, and further south at Kunga Island. The birds can dive in excess of 320 kilometres per hour!

Talunkwan Island, midway between Vertical Point and Tanu, is an eyesore. Vast areas of the forest have been razed.

There are no totems at Tanu to remind us that the greatest of the Haida carvers once lived here. Yet the native past is unmistakably present. You find it in the house pits and on the simply inscribed headstones: "In Memory of Charlie." And you find the creative spirit in Tanu in its magical setting. Sitting near the longhouse pits you savour the environment which inspired the Tanu artists. Your fingers luxuriate in the moss, thick and spongy, which carpets the forest floor. You hear music in the stream which splashes into the sea. Your eyes wander along the sandy beach out to the island-jewelled horizon. The evening sun paints the sky with rainbow colours. As night approaches the voices of the sea and forest soften. Listen carefully. You can almost hear the Tanu carvers at work on their totems.

Darwin Sound

One of the most scenic areas in the Queen Charlotte Islands is the coastline which parallels the barbed spine of Moresby Island's midsection. Other than a few handloggers who have nibbled at some tiny patches, the forests here are untouched. Every few miles an inlet incises the narrowing island, threatening to cut it in half. Without exception, a stream empties into each inlet, many draining mountain-walled lakes. The estuaries here teem with life: waterfowl, bear, deer and, unfortunately, carnivorous insects — millions of them. From mid-June to mid-August, bug-proof mesh is your only hope of sleep here. From the sea the alpine meadows and dramatic peaks of the San Cristoval Mountains are clearly visible. It is hard to believe that the mountains do not exceed 1,000 metres.

Anna Inlet, almost enclosed by land, is a popular anchorage with sailboat skippers. The remains of a boardwalk lead along the south side of the creek up to Anna Lake. There is no beach at the lake, but a fine view. Outside the gorge of Anna Inlet, a derelict truck bearing a 1969 licence plate marks the settlement of Lockeport, deserted long before that date. Lockeport, busiest in the first three decades of the century, once had a store, post office and cannery.

The abundance and diversity of nature in Darwin Sound would have delighted its namesake. Its shorelines fossils display the swirl of million-year-old scallop shells. An eagle seems to perch from every tree; Darwin Sound has one of the densest population of eagles in Canada. The dot on the chart in the middle of the sound, off the north end of Shuttle Island, is a veritable zoo: a seal colony, heron, gulls and oyster catchers. The latter will become hysterical, stomping their feet and crying unceasingly at your approach. A dogfish gulped our hook

Anna Inlet

here and as we hauled in our catch, our boat was surrounded by an armada of lip-licking sharks. The point on the northeast side of the island hides a mine shaft, cabin and an outhouse. Little gold was extracted here. At the southern end of Darwin Sound, on Lyell Island, we found the beach lined with surveyor's tape. What does this portend for the giant red cedars, some of the largest in the world, which are located here?

Lyell Island

The north coast of Lyell Island is heavily logged. A large camp operates at Powrivco Bay (named after the Powell River Company). Dodge Point at the north tip of the island is the most important nesting ground for the ancient murrelet on Canada's west coast.

One of the most spectacular watersheds on the Charlottes is at Windy Bay, on the east coast of Lyell Island. Windy Bay is one of the few places which genuinely deserves British Columbia's trademark —"supernatural." Few sitka spruce, hemlock, and cedar trees on the planet are larger than those found here. Some of the trunks are massive — more like walls than trees — and their lower branches are so thick that the forest appears to be growing horizontally. The ebb tides drain the protected shallow bay, exposing long bars of white sand. The returning flood tides smother the vast estuary with blue. Deer, oblivious to visitors, wander over the Haida house pits.

The Windy Creek watershed is prized not only for its aesthetic appeal, but also for its important scientific value. The watershed is one of the few in the Queen Charlotte Islands to have escaped man's intrusion. It has never been logged. It offers botanists, zoologists and ecologists a natural laboratory in which to study the Queen Charlottes' unique wilderness. The Islands Protection Society, a conservation group, wants to see all of the watershed protected and has widespread public support for this project. But further support is needed; a powerful forestry lobby wants to log portions of the watershed.

A sad example of how logging destroys the charm of a wilderness environment will be found just south of Windy Bay at Gate Creek. The beautiful creek and long beach once attracted many kayakers, but few camp here now. The nearby clear-cuts are too depressing.

In former times, the bay adjacent to Gate Creek was known as Windy Bay. Topographic map 103 B-C, issued by the British

Paddlers cross paths

Columbia Department of Environment, still indicates Windy Bay as next to Gate Creek, when in fact it is the bay immediately north which is now known as Windy Bay.

The east coast of Lyell Island can be tricky paddling territory. Winds and tidal currents can create high seas. Along the Tar Islands look for seals, oozing tar and agates.

Hotspring Island and Surrounding Islands

There is one more prize in this area: Hotspring Island. A series of hot springs of varying temperatures (from hot to very hot) bubble out of the rocks on the southwest corner of the island, the very corner which has the magnificent views across the water to the San Cristoval Mountains. There are three bath tubs, a miniature cement pool that can accommodate a half dozen soakers, and a host of natural pools formed in the intertidal rocks. A nearby cabin offers protection in the rain. There is no reliable source of fresh water on the island.

Like Hot Springs Cove on Vancouver Island, Hotspring Island is a social place, but the gathering here is somehow more homogeneous, more connected to the sea: fishermen, kayakers, long-distance sailboaters. A campfire dinner becomes a banquet. A fisherman donates a halibut or salmon, divers contribute abalone and scallops, someone steams freshly picked glasswort, maybe a native offers some herring roe-on-kelp. Add to that a spoonful from each of a half dozen pots, a communal bottle of wine and the setting sun over Juan Perez Sound, and you have cuisine that no gourmet restaurant could match.

The Bischof Islands and Murchison Island have full-time residents, some of whom are growing weary of kayak visitors. "The questions are always the same." The Haida once inhabited House Island and also the bay east of Andrew Point on Ramsay Island. On the south coast of the latter island, look for wild goats and sea caves.

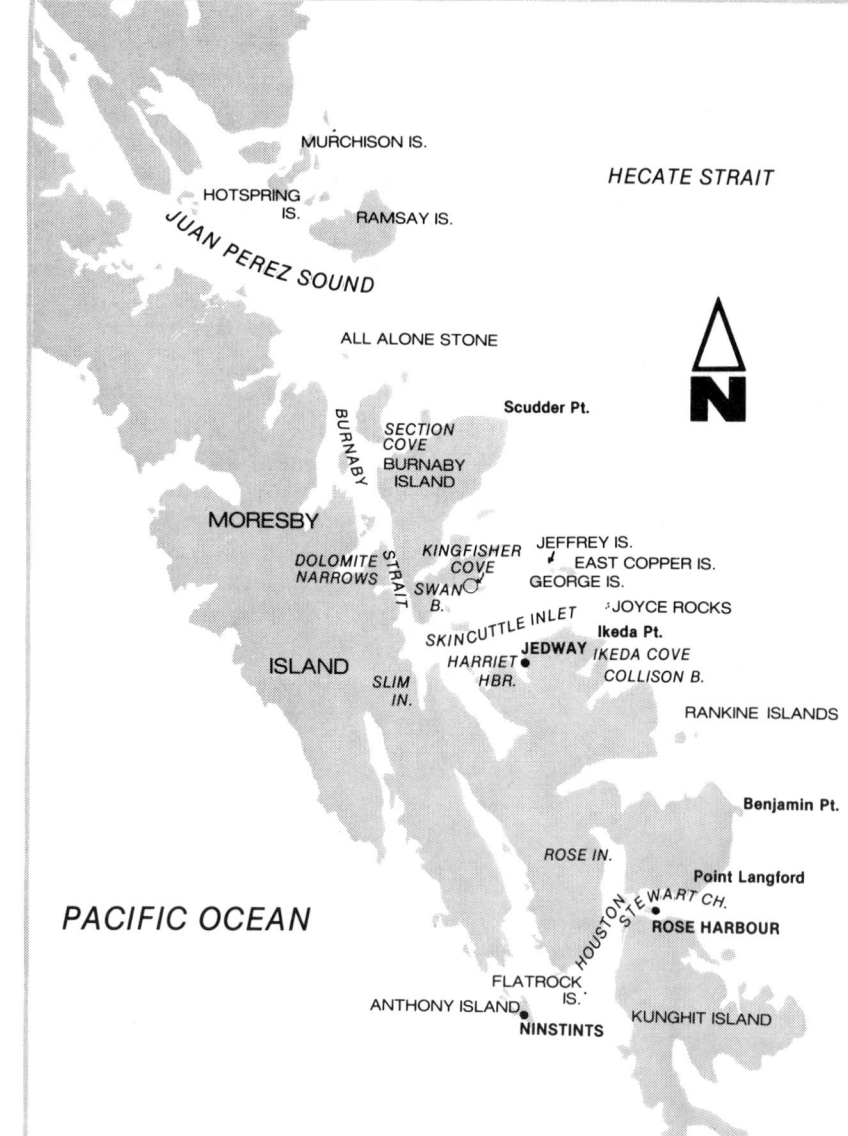

MURCHISON IS.

HECATE STRAIT

HOTSPRING IS.

RAMSAY IS.

JUAN PEREZ SOUND

ALL ALONE STONE

Scudder Pt.

N

BURNABY

SECTION COVE

BURNABY ISLAND

MORESBY

JEFFREY IS.

EAST COPPER IS.

DOLOMITE NARROWS

KINGFISHER COVE

GEORGE IS.

STRAIT

SWAN B.

JOYCE ROCKS

SKINCUTTLE INLET

Ikeda Pt.

ISLAND

HARRIET HBR.

JEDWAY

IKEDA COVE

COLLISON B.

SLIM IN.

RANKINE ISLANDS

Benjamin Pt.

ROSE IN.

Point Langford

HOUSTON STEWART CH.

PACIFIC OCEAN

ROSE HARBOUR

FLATROCK IS.

ANTHONY ISLAND

KUNGHIT ISLAND

NINSTINTS

MORESBY ISLAND — SOUTH

HOWE BAY

WOODRUFF BAY

0   5   10ⁿ·ᵐ·

Cape St. James

Moresby Island — South

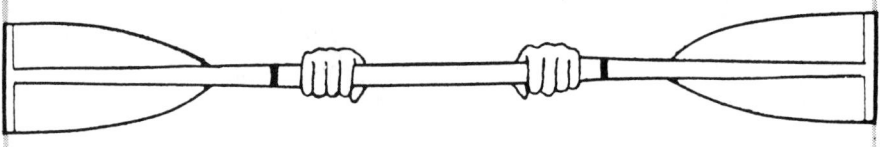

Area 20

Attractions: Anthony Island, the finest example of the west coast native heritage. Exceptionally rich sea bird life. The vast, unspoiled south Moresby and Kunghit Island wilderness. Challenging paddling.

Access: You can paddle from Sandspit or Queen Charlotte City all the way south to Anthony Island and back, but most kayakers will charter or hitch a ride on a fishing or pleasure boat or charter a float plane for one leg of the journey.

Seascape: Sheltered waters and open seas. Swell common on the southeast coast of Moresby. Houston Stewart Channel is generally tranquil. Three mile open water crossing to Anthony Island.

Hazards: Tide rips and standing waves at three locations: Scudder Point on the northeast tip of Burnaby Island, Benjamin Point on the eastern-most point of Moresby Island, and Point Langford at the eastern entrance to the Houston Stewart Channel. Shellfish beds at Dolomite Narrows are poisonous, due to the red tide.

Season: May to September. Mildest in July and August.

Length: 8 to 14 days, one-way from Hotspring Island to Anthony Island.

Camping: Plenty of shoreline camping sites. To visit Anthony Island you require two separate permits: one from the Indian band office at Skidegate and the other from the regional office of the B.C. Parks and Outdoor Recreation Division in Smithers.

Charts: 3808 Juan Perez Sound   1:37,500
3809 Carpenter Bay to Burnaby Island   1:37,500
3825 Cape St. James to Houston Stewart
       Channel   1:40,000
3853 Cape St. James to Cumshewa Inlet
       and Tasu Sound   1:150,000

Queen Charlottes

Introduction

As the Queen Charlottes taper southwards, their rugged topography softens. Fondled by a dozen inlet fingers, the delicate landscape of south Moresby or "Gaawa Hanas" as the Haida called it, has an almost mystical aura. Nature vibrates with an extraordinary profusion of life: bears, deers, whales, sea lions, halibut, salmon, cod, a high concentration of shellfish and sea birds, massive evergreens and a host of unique flora. For eons man harvested this bounty with great respect, enshrining this veneration in the animal carvings still visible today on the totems at the abandoned village of Ninstints on Anthony Island.

White man has visited south Moresby only intermittently, but long enough to do great harm to the environment. The depletion of the sea otter population, the near extinction of the whales and the decimation of the native people through diseases, all occurred during a very brief contact with white man. And further environmental damage may be imminent. A forestry company wants south Moresby's timber. In spite of anxious calls for the protection of this area, the provincial government has failed to act. Yet south Moresby is to the west coast of Canada what Stanley Park is to Vancouver — a priceless sanctuary. The Islands Protection Society, the native community and outdoor enthusiasts from all over the province hope that the same wisdom and foresight which led to the creation of Stanley Park in the midst of a growing city will soon inspire the government to preserve the south Moresby wilderness.

South Moresby's remoteness is one of its main attractions, but this makes getting there and back difficult, unless your boat can be flown in and out. Charter flights can be arranged from Sandspit to Murchison Island (near Hotspring Island), Burnaby Narrows, Rose Harbour, or wherever else a float plane can land. Or charter or hitch a ride south with a boat from Queen Charlotte City. Marine traffic south of Hotspring Island is very sparse. Another option is to paddle the entire trip from Sandspit to Anthony Island and back. A round trip requires a minimum of three weeks. A large group might consider chartering a helicopter in Sandspit to make food drops at designated spots along the route.

218

Modern warriors?

Juan Perez Sound and Burnaby Strait

A dip in the hot tubs on Hotspring Island (see page 214) is the best way to start or finish a trip to south Moresby. Juan Perez Sound is completely exposed to southeast winds; cross it in the early morning. Of all the thousands of names on the charts on Canada's west coast, our favourite is found in Juan Perez Sound: "All Alone Stone." Further south, Section Cove on the northeast coast of Burnaby Island is the site of an extremely lucrative herring roe-on-kelp fishery that operates for only six weeks every year, in early spring. At spawning time herring are collected into nets that are suspended in the water from floating logs. The herring deposit their roe on kelp fronds which dangle into the net. The seaweed caviar is removed from the water and dried, eaten raw or quick fried. Dipped in oolichan oil (sesame oil is an excellent substitute), it is ambrosia. The principal market for this delicacy is in Japan.

The shellfish beds of Dolomite Narrows (also known as Burnaby Narrows) are among the richest of the Pacific coast. Unfortunately, the bivalves here are frequently contaminated with the red tide. The narrows dry at low tide, exposing the forbidden bonanza on the seabed. The peculiar grey discs which litter the bottom, holed in the middle as if they were formed around a jar, look distinctly artificial. In fact, they are the egg cases of moon snails. Squatters' cabins dot the shoreline near Dolomite Narrows.

Skincuttle Inlet

Swan Bay, around the corner from Dolomite Narrows, is also inhabited. Here a couple built a seven metre sailing boat entirely from driftwood.

In the 1860's scores of copper prospectors explored the shores of Skincuttle Inlet. They dug mine shafts at Burnaby Island west of Kingfisher Cove, at Skincuttle Island, George Island and East Copper Island. The old shafts and tailings are still visible.

Jeffrey and East Copper Islands are ecological reserves and government regulations prohibit landing here without a permit. A high concentration of sea birds (over 13,000 pairs including Cassin's auklets, ancient murrelets, fork-tailed storm petrels and Leach's storm petrels) nest on these islands. The auklets and murrelets have a very strange method of landing. Returning at dusk from their long day at sea, these birds simply fold their wings and crash-land into the woods like a kamikaze pilot. They tumble to the ground and skurry into subterranean condominiums. An evening observer standing near such nests is likely to be hit by these feathery balls.

Watch for treacherous, usually submerged rocks east and north of the Copper Islands. Paddle cautiously near Scudder Point, on the north tip of Burnaby Island, as the tidal current can build dangerous seas. Gulls seem to hold a perpetual convention at Joyce Rocks, at the mouth of Skincuttle Inlet. Look for seals here.

Jedway and Ikeda Cove

The turn of the century saw a flurry of activity at Harriet Harbour. By 1907, a sizable community of hopeful copper prospectors had settled here. On the southwest corner of the harbour, a mill was constructed to cut the timber for mine shafts. A store, a post office, even a hotel operated here. Archie Ikeda, a fisherman, found a copper outcropping near his anchorage at the head of the cove that now bears his name. He was one of the very few to actually ship copper out of the Charlottes, and became a rich man in the process. A wireless station was installed at Ikeda Point and a line connected it with the Ikeda mine and Jedway hotel. By 1920, the supply of hope and copper expended, not a soul remained. In 1961, an iron ore open pit mine resurrected Jedway, this time on the east side of Harriet Harbour, and disembowled a hillside. The townsite was razed when the mine closed in 1968. Today, there are a few reminders of man's past industry. The stone wireless building at Ikeda Point is well-camouflaged in the forest. At the head of Ikeda Cove there are some rotten timbers and rusted mining rails. A rough trail leads up to the Jedway mining scar.

Collison Bay to Houston Stewart Channel

Walk back into the hushed rain forests along the many creeks that open onto this coastline. The huge, toppled evergreens reveal the wind's mighty power. The sand or pebble flats beside the streams are excellent spots for a sauna, constructed with saplings and tarps.

The Rankine Islands have been designated as an ecological reserve to protect the over 27,000 pairs of sea birds that nest here. Landing on these islands without a permit is not allowed.

Benjamin Point, the eastern-most extremity of Moresby Island, has a pair of crescent beaches, one facing north, the other south. Grass flats and a few decomposing house beams are the most obvious reminders of the Haida who once lived here. It is safest to paddle around the point at slack tide. The tide rips are especially dangerous when the winds and tides collide.

Room-sized boilers, gear mechanisms, decayed piles, fragments of whale bones and maybe even a pastel-tinted opium bottle constitute the beach-side monument to the whaling station which operated at Rose Harbour between 1910 and 1946. At the height of production, over 100 men worked here. Rose Harbour is one of the very rare pieces of private property in the southern Queen Charlotte Islands. In 1978, a group of Queen Charlotte Islanders bought this remote real estate. The garden and A-frame cabin which they have built portend a new order for Rose Harbour. To the local residents, Rose Harbour's main virtue is its seclusion; respect their desire for privacy.

If the seas do not allow excursions out into the open Pacific, there is much territory to explore in sheltered Houston Stewart Channel and Rose Inlet. The islands and flats at the end of Rose Inlet seem to catch the flotsam of the Pacific Ocean. The islands at the western entrance to the Houston Stewart Channel are noteworthy sea bird colonies. Look for the tufted puffins on aptly-named Flatrock Island.

The waters surrounding Kunghit Island are very rarely explored. They are too wild. But there is much here to reward sea kayakers. Highlights are the exceptionally beautiful, long beaches at Woodruff and Howe Bay. A beachcomber could spend many happy days here. The Cape St. James lighthouse promises human company and a weather report, but landing there is difficult due to the treacherous tide rips and heavy seas.

Anthony Island

In addition to the Indian band and Parks Division permits which you require to visit Anthony Island, you must get the permission of the caretaker who resides there permanently in the summer, if you want to camp on the island. Be sure to carry the maximum load of drinking water to the island as you will find only brown, though potable water from a small spring.

Leaving Houston Stewart Channel you must cross three miles of open ocean to Anthony Island. We had to struggle through a gale that was determined to send us to China. Upon reaching the protected cove on the eastern coast of the island we were greeted by a whole village, but a silent, unmoving one — a village of totem poles. The Haida deserted this settlement, called Ninstints, a century ago, but their handsomely carved totems still uphold the native spirit.

The natural life at Anthony Island is almost as impressive as the man-made monuments. The Haida named the island "Sgungwai," meaning "red cod island" because of the abundance of that species in the nearby waters. Kayakers with wet suits will be rewarded with abalone and scallops. Bird watchers will love Anthony Island. Over 35,000 pairs of sea birds — at least nine species including the horned and tufted puffin and the rhinoceros auklet — nest on the island and on the Anthony Islets offshore. The latter are within an ecological reserve. The cliffs south of Ninstints are an excellent place to observe the sea birds. Many nest in the ground, which explains the countless holes here.

You could spend many days exploring this multi-faceted island. You will find grassy fields, rain forests, deep caves, wave-splattered

Photos: Courtesy of the British Columbia Provincial Museum, Victoria, British Columbia

Anthony Island 1901

Anthony Island 1980's

beaches and mud flats. Beachcombers are sure to find something of interest swept in from the Pacific.

Anthony Island is a special place on this planet and deserves its UNESCO designation as an International Heritage Site. And for kayakers it has special importance, for it encapsulates the west coast paddling experience, the harmony of the land, the sea and man.

APPENDICES

Appendix A

Kayak Sailing and Kayak Kiting

Kayak Sailing

Sailing is one of the most delightful aspects of sea kayaking. It gives tired arm muscles a chance to rest and offers your mind a stimulating game, played with the changing wind and sea. Best of all, sailing affords silent propulsion, enabling the kayaker to locate and observe marine mammals whose husky inhalations are often obscured by the splash of paddles.

Few rigid kayaks are designed to accommodate sailing gear. On the other hand, most collapsible kayaks have the necessary fittings to hold a mast and rudder. The rudder is mounted at the stern of the boat and is controlled by foot pedals in the cockpit. Some boats have attachments on either side of the boat to which leeboards are fastened. All touring kayakers, no matter what type of boat they are paddling, have the necessary gear at hand to jury-rig a sail. Stretch a ground sheet or tent fly between paddles or tree branches and hold the rig aloft. This technique is most efficient when two or more boats are rafted together.

If your boat can accommodate a mast and rudder assembly, there are two basic sail designs which you can use: triangular or square. The triangular sails of the modern sloop or cat rigs are the most aerodynamically efficient, allowing the kayak to sail not just downwind and across the wind, but also closed hauled, that is, at an angle to the wind. We have found, however, that it is rarely practical to sail the kayak close hauled. Even when the kayak is fitted with leeboards it is faster to lower the sails and paddle.

The square sail (see front cover) is much more stable in most weather conditions than its triangular counterpart. The square sail has an approximately equal amount of area on either side of the mast, whereas the entire area of the triangular sails is on one side of the mast or the other, depending on the tack of the boat. Wind shifts can toss the triangular sail from side to side, which can easily capsize a kayak. Square sails can only be used when running before the wind or at a slight angle off it. Square sails, unlike triangular sails, cannot be sailed on a "reach," that is, at a 90° angle across the wind. This is not a serious disadvantage as the mountainous topography of the west

Kayak sailing

coast funnels the wind up and down the inlets and channels and rarely across them. Square sail rigs are easily made. Simply sew a sleeve at the opposite ends of the sail material (cloth, dacron, canvas) and insert into the sleeves appropriate lenghts of bamboo sticks or aluminum tubing, which become the booms. A telescoping boat hook makes a good mast. Fasten the upper boom so that it can rotate about the top of the mast. You can control the sail via lines attached to either side of the lower boom.

The kayak sailor must be able to quickly reef the sails or take them down. When winds exeed 12 to 15 knots it is generally only safe to have a small area of sail exposed to the wind. Both square and triangular sails are reefed by wrapping the sail around the lower boom. If your triangular sailing rig includes a jib, it is advisable to be able to remove the jib from the cockpit. This cannot be done if the jib is fastened to a fitting at the bow of the boat, as is common with many sailing rigs. A better arrangement is to run a line from the lower leading corner of the jib through the bow fitting to the cockpit. This way, not only can the jib be taken into the cockpit if necessary, but also the height of the jib, when hoisted, can be adjusted via the jib's halyard and the line to the bow fitting.

Sails are invariably under-utilized if they cannot be put up easily while at sea. For this reason, we usually paddle with the mast in position and the sails furled around the booms and fastened to the deck. The gear can be hoisted the moment favourable winds arise, without fumbling for the gear underneath the spray cover. A disadvantage with this procedure is that the sails are perpetually wet, which will hasten their deterioration. Moreover, unless properly fastened, the sails can be easily lost overboard or can obstruct paddling or rescue procedures.

It must be emphasized that a kayak is most unstable when under sail. An inexperienced sailor can capsize a kayak very easily. Before sailing your kayak, you should have a basic understanding of sailing theory and technique. It is essential to practice and experiment with the sails in safe, familiar waters before using them while touring. Remember that under touring conditions, your kayak will be ballasted with your camping gear and food; your kayak will handle much differently when sailed without such ballast. Your practice sessions with the sails should include rescue procedures. Righting a boat which has a mast in position and sailing gear attached can be considerably more difficult than righting a kayak which is not so encumbered.

Kayak Kiting

Kites, like sails, offer the kayaker an effortless and sometimes thrilling ride. Made from nylon fabric and having no rigid components, a kite can be rolled and stowed into a very small space. Besides pulling your boat, the colourful high-flying kite can be used to attract attention in an emergency. The few kayakers who have experimented with kites are extremely enthusiastic about the potential of kayak kiting. Leroy Nordby of Seattle is an authority on kayak kiting and the following discussion draws heavily on his experience.

Parafoils are the kites best suited to kayak kiting due to their great lift and pull. Numerous parafoil kites are on the market. For most kayaks, the optimum kite size is approximately one metre wide and 1.5 metres long. Larger kites are too unwieldy to manage from a

Photo: Will Nordby

Kayak kiting

kayak cockpit. Along with the kite you will need at least 100 metres of braided nylon line of at least 75 to 100 kilogram-test. The kite's line is fastened directly to a cleat or deckline on the boat or can be threaded through a pulley at the bow of the boat before being secured to the hull.

It takes considerable practice to launch and fly the kite from a kayak. Experience will teach how to fly the kite to maximize its pulling capability. The kite will generally fly at an angle of 60° off the water. You can travel directly downwind or at a 25° angle either side of downwind. If the winds are strong you may find it difficult and sometimes impossible to pull the kite down by hand. You must have some mechanism to release the kite's line from its fastening on the boat. Have your knife handy if you have no such mechanism. Upon release, the kite will lose its loft and fall to the sea, where it can be retrieved and put aboard.

It is essential that kiting kayakers experiment with their kites before using them under touring conditions.

Appendix B

(All numbers in brackets are telephone numbers; the area code is 604.)

Government Agencies

Canadian Coast Guard Radio
Stations:
Alert Bay (974-5413)
Bull Harbour (Radio
Campbell River)
Comox (339-3613)
Prince Rupert (624-9009)
or (624-1503)
Sandspit (637-5311)
Vancouver (270-7411)
Victoria (642-3431)

Environment Canada:
Weather Reports (270-7411)

Federal Department of
Fisheries & Oceans:
Bella Bella (957-2312)
Campbell River (287-2102)
Kitimat (632-6158)
Nanaimo (753-4181)
Port Hardy (949-6422)
Port Alberni (724-0195)
Powell River (485-9621)
Prince Rupert (624-9137)
Queen Charlotte
City (559-4413)
Sandspit (637-5340)
Vancouver (666-3169)
Victoria (388-3252)

British Columbia Provincial
Museum
601 Belleville Street
Parliament Buildings
Victoria, B.C.
V8V 1X4

Ministry of Lands, Parks
and Housing,
Ecological Reserves Unit
1019 Wharf Street
Victoria, B.C.
V8W 2Y9

Ministry of Lands, Parks
and Housing,
Parks and Outdoor
Recreation Division
1019 Wharf Street
Victoria, B.C.
V8W 2Y9

Parks and Outdoor
Recreation Division
Skeena Region
Bag 5000
3793 Alfred Street
Smithers, B.C.
V0J 2N0

Pacific Rim National Park
Box 280
Ucluelet, B.C.
V0R 3A0

Indian Band Councils

Bella Bella Band
Box 880
Waglisla, B.C.
V0T 1Z0
(957-2381)

Ehattesaht Band
Box 98,
Zeballos, B.C.
V0P 2A0
(Radio Zeballos 284)

Gitlakdamix Band
New Aiyansh, B.C.
V0J 1A0
(633-2215)

Hesquiaht Band
Box 238
Tofino, B.C.
V0R 2Z0
(Radio Tofino,
   Boat Basin 98077)

Kincolith Band
Kincolith, B.C.
V0V 1B0
(Radio Terrace,
Nass, N 694902)

Kyuquot Band
Kyuquot, B.C.
V0P 1J0
(Radio Kyuquot, N 710147)

Mamalillikulla Band
39 - 300 Robron Road
Campbell River, B.C.
V9W 5P2
(923-3139)

Nuchatlaht Band
Box 407
Tahsis, B.C.
V0P 1X0

Skidegate Band
R.R. # 1, Box 1
Queen Charlotte City, B.C.
V0T 1S0
(559-4496)

Wilderness Conservation Groups

Gambier Island:
Gambier Island Preservation
Society,
Box 46331, Station G
Vancouver, B.C.
V6R 4G6

Meares Island:
Friends of Clayoquot Sound
Box 503
Tofino, B.C.
V0R 2Z0

Princess Louisa Inlet:
Greenpeace
2623 West Fourth Avenue
Vancouver, B.C.
V6K 1P8

Robson Bight:
Robson Bight Preservation
Committee,
Box 48
Port McNeill, B.C.
V0N 2R0
or:
Sierra Club of Western
Canada
536A Yates St.,
Victoria, B.C.
V8P 1S4

South Moresby:
Islands Protection Society
Box 302
Masset, B.C.
V0T 1M0

Tahsish-Kwois Watershed:
Kyuquot-Tahsish Committee
Kyuquot, B.C.
V0P 1J0

Windy Bay:
Islands Protection Society
Box 302
Masset, B.C.
V0T 1M0

Transportation

Marine:
Alberni Marine
Transportation Ltd.
Box 188
Port Alberni, B.C.
V9Y 7M7
(723-6122 - office)
(723-8313 - deck)

British Columbia Ferry
Corporation Ltd.
1045 Howe Street
Vancouver, B.C.
V6Z 2A9
(669-1211)

Coast Ferries Ltd.
1400 E. Kent Street
Vancouver, B.C.
V5P 4N8
(321-6833)

Nootka Sound Service Ltd.
Box 28
Port Alberni, B.C.
V9Y 7M6
(723-3132 - office)
(283-2325 - dock)

Air:
Air BC
Head Office
4680 Cowley Crescent
Richmond, B.C.
V7B 1C1
(273-2464)
Bella Bella (957-2285)
Bella Coola (982-2232)
Campbell River (287-2419)
Nanaimo (753-1255)
Port Hardy (949-6353)
Vancouver (263-2877)
Victoria (388-5151)

CP Air
Head Office
#1 - Bentall Centre
505 Burrard Street
Vancouver, B.C.
V7X 1M3
(682-1411)
Prince Rupert (624-9181)
Terrace (635-7111)

Minstrel Air
Kelsey Bay (282-3765)
Alert Bay (974-5811)

North Coast Air
Box 610
Prince Rupert, B.C.
V8J 3R5
(627-1351)

Pacific Western Airlines
Head Office
Suite 2700
700 - 2nd Street S.W.
Calgary, Alberta
T2P 2W2
Port Hardy (949-6412)
Sandspit (637-5388)
Vancouver (684-6161)
Victoria (388-5191)

Trans-Provincial Airlines
Box 280
Prince Rupert, B.C.
V8J 3P8
(627-1341)
Trans-Provincial Airlines
Box 224
Sandspit, B.C.
V0T 1T0
(637-5355)

233

Miscellaneous

Crown Zellerbach
Box 470
Sandspit, B.C.
V0T 1T0
(637-5323)

MacMillan Bloedel
Hecate Division
Box 233
Sandspit, B.C.
V0T 1T0
(637-5391)

Museum of Anthropology
University of British
Columbia
6393 N.W. Marine Drive
Vancouver, B.C.
V6T 1W5
(228-3825)

Vancouver Public Aquarium
Stanley Park
(685-3364)

Vancouver Public Library
Main Branch
750 Burrard Street
Vancouver, B.C.
V6Z 1X5
(665-2280)

Vancouver Ocean Touring &
Kayak Association
For current address, contact
the following:
Canoe Sport B.C.
1200 Hornby Street
Vancouver, B.C.
V6Z 2E2
(687-3333)

Ocean Kayaking Association
of B.C.
c/o Box 356
Victoria, B.C.
V8W 2N2

Index

The Authors

John Ince, a resident of the west coast for 25 years, is an experienced dinghy sailor and a keen outdoors enthusiast. Hedi Kottner, a native of Munich, West Germany, came to Canada in 1979 after three years of travel in Europe, Asia, Africa and South America. The authors spent two years exploring Canada's west coast in their kayak. Their articles and photographs about sea kayaking have appeared in numerous publications in Canada, the United States and Europe. When not kayak touring, John Ince practices law in Vancouver and Hedi Kottner teaches German and works as a freelance writer and photographer.